Praise for *Life of Your Dreams*

"*Life of Your Dreams* is more than a book—it's a blueprint for achieving greatness in every area of your life. Mark's journey from schoolteacher to self-made entrepreneur is proof that dreaming big and taking action can create extraordinary results. His insights and lessons on mindset, leadership, and perseverance will inspire you to rewrite your own story and step into your full potential."

—Lewis Howes, *New York Times* Bestselling
Author, Host of *The School of Greatness*

"Mark Pentecost is a great AMERICAN story as his book will INSPIRE, MOTIVATE, and show you how he and his wife, Cindy, chased their dreams and became WINNERS in the 'GAME of LIFE.' Mark is so special because once he gained fantastic financial success from building his corporate endeavor IT WORKS! GLOBAL, he utilized his success to help many. The Pentecosts have hearts of gold and have helped me tremendously by raising lots of money for pediatric cancer research through the V Foundation. Yes, this read will encourage YOU to chase your DREAMS. I close by simply stating MARK and CINDY are AWESOME, BABY, with a capital A!"

—Dick Vitale, ESPN Sportscaster
and Motivational Speaker

"When you read this book, you will enter the world of a winner. It's packed full of keys to winning against all odds when life hits hard. Mark Pentecost is one of the most inspiring American success stories. This magnificent book will plant dream seeds in your thought life that will become the road map to your dream life."

—Jentezen Franklin, Senior Pastor, Free Chapel,
New York Times Bestselling Author

"This book is for anyone who has ever needed permission to chase their dreams and make a positive impact on the world. Whether you consider yourself a dreamer or not, this book is for you. Mark has lived these lessons firsthand and shares them in a way that deeply resonates. My friend Mark is truly the embodiment of the American Dream and one of the greatest Americans of our time."

—Brooke L. Rollins, Secretary of Agriculture,
Founder of America First Policy Institute

"Excluding private equity and Silicon Valley, Mark Pentecost's journey from a teacher and coach to achieving a billion-dollar milestone at a remarkable speed stands second to none. Mark's vision and strategic decision-making have consistently elevated him and his company to new heights. His story is living proof that the American Dream is alive through grit, faith, and commitment."

—Don M. Hamilton, Director of Sales,
Ultra Wealth/Family Office,
Huntington National Bank

"This book is an empowering guide to taking control of your destiny and designing the life you truly desire. With practical exercises, inspiring stories, and profound insights, it offers readers the tools to break free from limitations and step into their full potential. A must-read for anyone ready to create lasting change and live with purpose and passion!"

—Dr. Caroline Leaf, Clinical and Research
Neuroscientist, Bestselling Author

LIFE
of
YOUR
DREAMS

LIFE
of
YOUR
DREAMS

HOW TO TAKE YOUR FAMILY, FUN, AND
FINANCIAL FREEDOM TO A WHOLE 'NOTHA LEVEL

MARK PENTECOST

Published by Mission Driven Press, an imprint of Forefront Books, Nashville, Tennessee.
Distributed by Simon & Schuster.

Library of Congress Control Number: 2025900971

Print ISBN: 978-1-63763-423-3
E-book ISBN: 978-1-63763-424-0

Cover Design by George Stevens
Interior Design by PerfecType, Nashville, TN

Printed in the United States of America
25 26 27 28 29 30 [LSC] 10 9 8 7 6 5 4 3 2 1

DEDICATION

*To my wife, Cindy, whose love and faith
have allowed me to always dream bigger
while keeping God and our family first.*

*To my children, Kami, Kindsey, and
Kyler, who have taken my dreaming
and legacy to a whole 'notha level.*

*May my grandkids, both those I know and
those I've yet to meet, carry forward the power
of dreaming big. God placed you in our family
because you are capable of more—of being
more, and of helping others to become more.*

*Dream big, chase those dreams, and let
your journey create positive change.*

ACKNOWLEDGMENTS

Thank you to all my friends and family who have gone on this journey with me and made it legendary. A special shout-out to Kindsey and Kyler for making this book come to life.

CONTENTS

Born to Dream

I just wanted more cash than bills.

Hi, I'm Mark Pentecost, professional dreamer. And I'm on a mission to empower people to live the lives of their dreams.

What is a professional dreamer? Well, I'm glad you asked. My job is to help you take your dreams to *a whole 'notha level*. I used to think a dreamer was someone who sat around wishing but not doing. Now I know a dream is a vision, a stirring within that moves you to act. As you step out to follow it, you dream again, then again, until one day you look up and say, "Wow! How did I get here?"

My own journey took me from high school teacher and coach to millionaire to billionaire. When I started, all I wanted was more cash than bills as I struggled to make ends meet for our family. Along the way, I always believed in the American Dream. Yet as I listened to so many people just like me, I started to wonder if I was the only one who wanted more but felt stuck in day-to-day survival mode. The more people I talked to, the more I realized a lot of other people felt stuck too.

As a math teacher for sixteen years, I often listened to frustrated coworkers in the teachers' lounge who felt unfulfilled and became jaded over time as their dreams passed them by. When I stepped away from coaching and teaching to start my own business, I met so many people who wanted more freedom and flexibility but didn't think they could risk pursuing it and provide for the people they love. So, they stayed stuck.

As I grew my business, I met fellow entrepreneurs and business leaders who set out to pursue bigger purposes, but somewhere along the way, they got stuck in the day-to-day, their fears keeping them feeling safe but miserable. When I hung out with leaders who usually inspire others to be and to do more, I realized they had the same struggle—all too often, they settled for playing it safe instead of daring to dream.

I heard this same story everywhere I went, from hardworking nurses in cancer wards to actors and set designers I met while filming a Western movie on our cattle ranch. They all told me the same thing: They felt stuck but didn't know what to do about it.

With all these people, it didn't matter what their background was. It didn't matter if they were nineteen, thirty-five, or fifty-two. And it didn't matter what they did for a living. Regardless of whether they were college students or attorneys, actors or pastors, nurses or influencers, athletes or movie set builders, all of them said the same thing: They just felt stuck.

Why did *you* start reading this book? Maybe you feel stuck too. Maybe somebody at some point told you to be "realistic," and you stopped listening to that part of yourself that has been growing more and more discontent. So you let your dreams slip away without even realizing it. *Oh, I can always go back someday,* you told yourself. But "someday" just never came. Now, the harder you work, the more your dreams get pushed to the back burner.

If you're like me, you probably did all the things you were "supposed" to do. You went to college or invested in training that was supposed to guarantee success. You may have taken out school loans because everyone said you'd make more money that way. You wanted to dream of more, but then life happened. Your significant other arrived. Then maybe a child or several children came along. Soon you found yourself surrounded by people you love who need you—but you also found yourself going deeper into debt, trading time for dollars, and feeling a little less alive every day. And now your life has gotten so busy that dreaming just feels like a luxury you can't afford.

Day after day, you roll out of bed in the morning and tumble back into it at night feeling stuck in a rut. You may still show a smiling face to everyone else, but on the inside you feel unsettled. To top it off, you feel guilty when you do think about how you feel. After all, you *do* want to be there for the people who depend on you. But sometimes you wish for more—more flexible time to spend with your family, more margin in life to focus on what's important to you, more financial freedom instead of debilitating debt, and more *fun* instead of what has come to feel like an endless grind.

Sound familiar? Believe me, I've felt that same frustration. At one point, I felt like I'd done everything I was supposed to do—went to college, got married, had kids—but I just wasn't getting ahead financially, and I had no time to do what I really wanted to do. I know the pain of feeling like your dream is slipping away a little bit more every single day—or even feeling like you're going backward. The more I worked, the more I fell behind. I loved my family and wanted to come through for them, but I just felt stuck—though a hunger for more kept stirring inside me.

For many years, I didn't know what to do about it as I continued to coach basketball and teach math. I just believed deep down that I was born to dream. And I believe the same is true for you.

THE DEPENDENCE DILEMMA

I believe we are all born to dream. We're wired to do it, just like breathing, eating, and sleeping. Dreaming comes naturally to everyone who enters this world. But behind the busyness of everyday life and the responsibilities of "adulting," many of us simply lose touch with our ability to dream—even though somewhere deep inside, we still sense a longing for something more.

It's as if something is keeping us from dreaming, causing us to ignore that stirring within. I call it the Dependence Dilemma. It's that feeling of being stuck between a rock and a hard place in life. It happens when life pressures seem to unite against you so that, no matter what moves you make, you just feel unable to get ahead.

On one side there's *the rock*—the people who *depend on you* to be there for them. Maybe you've got children to care for or parents who need your support—or both. So you feel like you couldn't possibly pursue what you really want to in life because that could take away time or resources from the people who count on you every day. And you think to yourself, *Wouldn't that be selfish of me?* Now, you don't mind that those you care about count on you to pay the bills, put a roof over their head, and drive them to dance class, doctor's appointments, and everything else. In fact, you wouldn't have it any other way. But how can you think about doing anything different when so many people depend on you? Truth be told, there are days when it can feel like you're carrying a massive rock all by yourself.

On the other side, there's *the hard place*—the things *you depend on* to bring home a paycheck and make ends meet. Let's face it, it's called a hard place for reason. You need to show up for that paycheck to pay your rent or mortgage, car payment, student loans, and everything in between. On top of it all, your job might provide other benefits you think your family needs like healthcare or childcare. You depend on the security of work and a paycheck to help you take care of all those people who depend on you. Lose the system, and the bottom falls out. You can't just let go of the people you care about because if you do, they'll suffer for it.

Maybe you're single and just want to be able to finally move out of your parents' basement—but the only affordable option is to split a smaller place with roommates. Maybe you've got children to care for, so you pick up a side gig to make a little extra cash to get ahead—but now your daughter wants to start dance lessons. Or you've finally paid off that credit card debt that's been hanging over your head for years—but you just found out your son needs braces. Maybe you love to travel and have been planning a romantic getaway for months—but now your car has started making strange noises that you know can't be good. Or maybe you just want more freedom and flexibility in your life—but your employer keeps increasing your responsibilities and your job is feeling more and more structured and controlling.

The specifics of the Dependence Dilemma will look different for everyone, but the common thread is that most days it feels like you've got no more room to dream. The worst part is that just when you think you might be finding a way out, something inevitably goes wrong. Every. Single. Time.

For many years when I was just trying to put food on the table for our kids, I drove pickup trucks that I patched together to keep running. After working a lot of side gigs, I finally managed to buy a sharp-looking pickup truck from my uncle. *We're finally getting ahead*, I thought. Just three weeks later, the noise began. When the mechanic gave me the diagnosis—"You need a completely new engine"—I felt a punch to the gut. Three weeks. That's all I got with my new truck.

So where do you feel the pressures of the Dependence Dilemma? What have been some of your own "punch-in-the-gut" moments? When was the last time you thought you were finally getting ahead before something unexpected happened, and you were right back to feeling stuck between the people who depend on you and the system you depend on to pay the bills? How does it all make you feel?

What I have found to be true is that these seemingly never-ending pressures can leave you thinking what so many other people have concluded: *Dreaming is just a luxury I can't afford.* If that's you, don't miss this: Despite the pressures you feel right now in the Dependence Dilemma, you still picked up this book. That's how I know you're ready for something different and, yes, for something more.

YOU ARE NOT ALONE

The first thing to know is that if you struggle to dream, you're not alone. A 2021 Gallup survey found that hope about the future and happiness in general is in decline.[1] In fact, hope in the US has dropped even lower than it was in 2020—when we were in the middle of a global pandemic. This is especially alarming because people who live with less of a reason to hope die sooner.[2] We're losing hope. We're not dreaming. And we're dying because of it. Something seems broken, as if we're not aligning with what we were born to do: dream.

If we are born to dream, it's no wonder that dreaming actually makes us physically healthier. A recent study found that people with a clear vision and dream were less likely to die sooner— by as much as 20 percent in men and 34 percent in women.[3] Other studies demonstrate that people who dream with purpose actually sleep better,[4] have lower chances of having a stroke,[5] and consistently feel better about themselves.[6]

So if dreaming helps us live better and longer lives and we are born to do it, why do we struggle to dream? As I've listened to the many people who feel stuck, I've heard a few reasons. See if you connect with any of these:

- **I don't feel worthy.** We often have a nagging feeling that we just don't deserve our dreams. That sense of unworthiness drags down our confidence levels because we think we simply aren't good enough.

- **I'm afraid to be disappointed.** The truth is, it is risky to put our dreams out there. What if—yet again—they don't come true? We all know what disappointment feels like, and it's easier to avoid it by just not dreaming.
- **I'm afraid to fail.** No one likes to fail, of course, but the fear of failure often leaves us in a worse place because it keeps us from trying for more—and then we end up feeling frustrated about it.
- **I think we can't afford to take risks.** Taking any sort of risk would affect more than just ourselves. We have people who depend on us at home and at work. For some of us, asking others to risk their stability and security just feels like too much. So we silence our dreams.
- **I don't believe different is possible.** When we feel like we carry the day-to-day weight of the world on our shoulders, it gets tough to imagine how life could be different. It's easy to get stuck in the rut of *what is* and not dare to dream about *what could be.*
- **I don't know where to start.** We don't get provided with an instruction manual when we're born for how to live our dreams, so it can feel like we just have to somehow figure it out. If we're already busy and overwhelmed,

how can we add yet another unknown to our
to-do list?

- **I struggle to see beyond today.** It's normal
  to focus on what is in front of us right now.
  So many of us live our lives based only on
  what we can see in the headlights right now.
  But dreaming is like driving with our bright
  lights finally turned on. When we reactivate our dreams, we suddenly see a host of
  options that were there all along.

If you relate to any of those struggles, you are
not alone. Unfortunately, not dreaming has become
normal. For so many people from every walk of life,
normal means grinding away every day but never
getting ahead. It means feeling unsettled and unfulfilled, even when everyone tells you there's something
wrong with your hunger for more.

But they are wrong. A dreamer can't help but
dream forward and hunger for more. The hunger you
have stirring within you doesn't mean something is
wrong with you; it actually means something is right
with you. You were born to dream.

That's why I chose to reject what the world told
me was normal and dared to dream again. If you,
too, are tired of settling for feeling stuck in life and
want to finally live the life of your dreams, I've got
great news: You can! As I took my own journey,

I discovered what I call—*drum roll, please*—the Dream Phenomenon.

DREAMERS OF THE DAY

The Dream Phenomenon is a way of seeing life that changes everything. When I began living it, I discovered that if I could do it, anyone could. Like I said, I went from teacher and coach to millionaire to billionaire, but I didn't write this book to brag—far from it. I remember all too well what it felt like to be stuck.

I just want you to know that when I talk about wanting to help you achieve your dreams, I'm not telling you a theory that I think *might* work. I'm telling you what *did* work. So many of those same people who once told me they felt stuck in life have followed the Dream Phenomenon. Now they have found freedom from the Dependence Dilemma and are living the lives of their dreams.

Wherever you are in life and whatever frustration you may be feeling, the Dream Phenomenon is the key to creating more opportunity and making a massive impact in the world. It is your invitation to make more money, finally get debt-free, and start building the kind of wealth that can change your destiny. It is your ticket to enjoying life more, to controlling your own story instead of letting others do it for you, and to doing more meaningful work that fills you up.

The Dream Phenomenon is a seven-step cycle that guides you to reconnect with your dreams and gives you the tools to take action and embrace a dreaming lifestyle. I'll show you how to deal with whatever comes your way, surround yourself with people who believe in you, and develop the ability to redream as you go. I guarantee you that whatever you dare to dream right now—no matter how big it may seem to you today—will come to feel like a stepping stone as your dreams grow.

When I talk about a *dream*, I'm talking about a vision for something that connects deeply with you personally. To paraphrase T. E. Lawrence, we were all born to dream, but not all choose to do it equally. Those who dream only by night awaken to find that it was only a wish. But dreamers of the day are dangerous because they act on their dreams with open eyes—*and they make them possible!* How cool would it be for you to become a dreamer of the day— to get really good at connecting the reality of where you are today with the possibility of what could be better tomorrow? That's what the Dream Phenomenon is all about.

Some people might dismiss dreamers as "pie-in-the-sky" folks who waste valuable time wishing. But a dream goes deeper than a wish; dreaming always implies *doing*. While a wish merely hopes for better, a dream pursues it. While a wish waits for power, a dream makes its own power. While a wish prefers comfort to work, a dream is what makes the work worth doing. And while wishing would prefer someone else do something for you, a dream moves you to own your own destiny.

One thing I know for sure is that if you never connect with your dreams, you will never realize them, guaranteed. They will always remain wishes unless you are willing to develop them. So, are you just hoping something better will somehow come your way, or are you taking focused action to develop your dreams of a better tomorrow? The choice is yours.

I realize your life circumstances may look challenging right now. Your story up to this point may be full of reasons why you should settle for normal. But by using the Dream Phenomenon, I *guarantee* you *can* leave normal behind and learn to dream at *a whole 'notha level!* In fact, my entire story is about learning to dream at *a whole 'notha level!*

What I don't want to hear from you is what I've heard from other people on my journey: *I wish I had joined you earlier to live the life of my dreams. Is it too late now?* No, it's never too late to start dreaming! But I don't want you to have any regrets. That's why I'm giving you the opportunity to join me now as a dreamer of the day.

In this book, I'll show you how you can live the life of your dreams. I believe in the power of *you*! *You* can achieve more. *You* can win more. *You* can do more of the things you want to do. Sure, you've got obstacles. We all do. Maybe you've tried and failed. Join the club. Maybe you feel like someone is holding you back, or maybe *you* are what is holding you back.

Just know this: The fact that you feel stuck right now is actually an invitation to set normal aside and step into a new path for your life.

Trust me, when you choose to become a dreamer, your life will change. For one thing, you'll have a lot of fun along the way. And that fun will spread because dreaming is contagious.

If you're ready to make your first move to become a professional dreamer like me, take action now. Simply turn the page.

And let me be the first to say, "Welcome to the club!"

Give Yourself Permission to Dream

People are often scared of doing the wrong thing when what they should be scared of is doing nothing.

I believe everyone has a Dream Muscle. I know, it might sound a little crazy, but dreams are really a lot like our physical muscles. And just like those muscles, your Dream Muscle needs to be used regularly to become stronger. As a result, the more you dream, the greater your capacity for dreaming becomes.

We're all born to dream, but then we get to choose: We can either take an Active path to strengthen our Dream Muscle, or we can slide down the Passive path and let our Dream Muscle weaken over time.

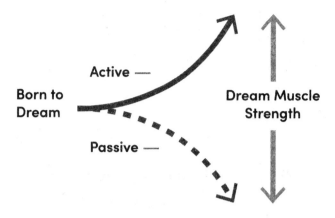

Maybe you don't even remember the last time you let yourself dream. If you haven't used your Dream Muscle in a while—or at all—trust me, it's still there. Even if it feels awkward at first, don't let that stop you. You need to condition yourself to dream even if it feels uncomfortable. This will soon become your *new* normal: allowing yourself to work your Dream Muscle long enough to see the result you want.

When you first start working out your Dream Muscle, it might feel like returning to the gym after years of not working out. At first, you *will* feel some resistance. That's enough to stop a lot of people, and it may have been enough to stop you in the past, but not anymore. Resistance is not a sign that you should quit; it's actually proof of your growth.

You *can* start today, with whatever dream feels right for you, to activate your Dream Muscle to reach heights you can only dare to imagine.

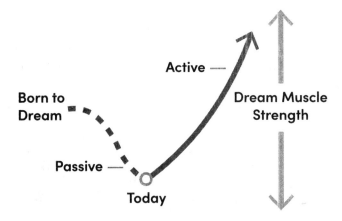

Even if exercising your Dream Muscle feels a little intimidating, you still feel that stirring inside, don't you? You hear that voice that keeps getting louder and louder until finally you realize it is you yelling, *I want to dream!*

Maybe you're like me when I first started dreaming, and all you can dare to dream for is more cash than bills. *Great! Start there.* Or maybe you are already clear about your dream destination. Maybe you want to make a drastic change in career to something you love. *If so, what are you waiting for?* Whatever your first dream might be, just give yourself permission to start.

THE ONE QUESTION

What is it you truly want that you simply don't have enough of right now? In other words, *why* do you want to dream?

When I was coaching and teaching, the better I did my job, the more it took away from what I really wanted. The more I poured myself into teaching, the more students talked about how much they enjoyed my classes—and the more students enrolled in them. That meant more homework to review, more report cards to complete, and more parent–teacher conferences to attend. Add in my coaching responsibilities, and soon my nine-to-five spilled over into every area of my life.

Don't get me wrong; I loved the students. I certainly wanted to help them. But with a family of five and bills to pay, I didn't feel like I was seeing the financial rewards for all my effort. No matter how hard I worked or how good a teacher I was, I only saw a small pay increase every year. I dreamed of a path that paid me for how well I delivered results and that didn't use all the time I longed to spend with the people I care about most.

Maybe you know how that feels. You got good grades and went to a good college so you could get a good job. Then, as your reward, you get to live a life where your time is almost completely dictated by an employer. You might get a decent paycheck and even some health insurance, but if you want to get paid more, you have to wait until your next annual review to *hopefully* get a small salary increase. Want to take time off for that dream vacation? It will be a while before you can "earn" enough vacation time.

I get it, believe me. Being born into the latter part of the boomer generation, I always heard that the way to succeed is to go to school and get a safe, secure job with benefits where you could stay for most of your career. For many years, this felt like the right path for my wife, Cindy, and me, but it couldn't silence the stirring within for something more.

We kept working our Dream Muscles without even realizing it. Almost by accident at the time, we put in the dream reps with side hustles and real estate deals. Little by little, our Dream Muscles grew, even when we weren't seeing the results we wanted right away. It turns out we were ahead of our time when we started working side gigs to find our own path toward our *why*.

The *why* behind my dream was the freedom to live a lifestyle full of opportunity, to enjoy time with my family, and to make more meaningful memories with them. I wanted to see my children laughing and playing as we took family vacations without worrying about whether the car would make the trip. I wanted to see the smile on my wife's face when I bought her the new car she deserved after trying to figure out how to make ends meet for so many years.

Why do *you* want to dream? Maybe you're like one young man I met who had his whole life in front of him. After spending time with me on a project, he realized he hadn't really gotten clear on *why* he needed to dream. Like a lot of younger people, he was so busy trying to make ends meet and get his career off the ground that he hadn't even realized he wasn't pursuing the things that really mattered to him. Once he became aware of it, he gave himself permission to live. You see, dreaming is contagious. This young man realized he could start dreaming and even dare to live the life he'd always wanted once he spent some time with someone who was actively dreaming—*me*.

Dreaming can become your legacy, too, as it did for a mom I met.

"Crystal" was in her late thirties. She was a single mom of three kids. She desperately wanted to create financial freedom so that she could better support her children. But up until that point of her life she hadn't figured out how to break free. She was trying, because she was working multiple jobs. But they weren't jobs where she got paid for her results, only for her time. And so she was exhausted. Like so many of us, she was trying to make ends meet but she had been falling short. But on this particular day a few years later, she had won an incentive trip with our company to come over to my house with a small group of her peers. We were sitting outside my house on the ocean looking at the beautiful water. I can still hear the rustling of the leaves of the palm trees outside and feel the breeze from the outdoor fan that we were sitting underneath. As we were wrapping up the meeting, Crystal came up to me and gave me the biggest hug and she started crying. I didn't know her all that well and so I was taken aback a little. I asked her, "Are you OK?"

Crystal looked up at me with tears in her eyes and she said, "Mark, you don't know this, but before I came here, I was really struggling in my life. I was struggling financially for sure, but I was struggling with something deeper than that. It had been a long time since I had allowed myself to have a dream. I gave up early on my dreams because I decided that I was just going to dedicate my life to my kids. But then something happened. One day I realized that my kids weren't dreaming. And when I thought about why, it dawned on me that the answer was obvious. It was because they didn't know how to dream. And the reason they didn't know how to dream is because they had never seen me do it. That day changed my entire life because I realized that it was one thing for me not to pursue my dreams because I thought it was safer for me to just be more responsible. But as a result of me not pursuing my dreams, my kids stopped pursuing theirs. And that was something that I was not OK with. And it was about that time that I met you and this team. Meeting you has been powerful for my life because it's enabled me to be surrounded by people who believe in me and who believe in chasing after what they want. Because of this environment, and because of my kids, I've started dreaming again . . . and so have my kids."

Crystal gave herself permission to dream again. Soon she paid off her debt and started her own business. Most importantly, her children began to dream—and her family's future changed forever.

Whatever your *why* may be, focus on it. It will inspire you to keep working your Dream Muscle so you can dream and dream and dream until the world calls you a visionary. Only you and I will know that you've become one of us—*a professional dreamer.*

WHAT'S HOLDING YOU BACK?

If you know your *why*, then why aren't you already daring to dream? It's time to get honest about what's holding you back and keeping you stuck in "normal" life. Often, it's the beliefs we tell ourselves about our situations that keep us from daring to dream. But your new normal involves giving yourself permission to think differently.

Even back when I was a rookie high school math teacher, I knew I wasn't cut out to be normal when Principal MacFalone told me he'd be coming by one of my classes to evaluate me. The class he chose was Math for Daily Living. It wasn't a secret that most of the students in that particular class didn't want to be there, so I suspected his expectations were low.

I could have chosen to be normal and see the visit as being about Principal MacFalone evaluating me. Instead, I chose to flip the narrative. I didn't want to be that teacher who called on students only to get nothing but crickets. I saw the visit as an opportunity to get the students engaged and help the entire class shine.

"Principal MacFalone is coming here to check us out," I told them, "and he wants to see if you know your stuff. I want to make you look as good as possible, so while he's here, raise your right hand if you know the answer to a question." They looked unimpressed with my plan. "And if you don't know the answer, raise your left hand." One by one, they started to snicker and smile. "Don't worry," I assured them, "I'll only call on you if you raise your right hand." They breathed a collective sigh of relief.

When the principal came, hand after hand shot up to question after question. Unfortunately, I saw almost all left hands a couple of times, so I had to think fast and say, "Oh, you all know it already. I'll just show you how to do it to keep my own skills sharp."

A couple hours after his visit, I heard the principal announce over the loudspeaker that all the faculty were to meet in the teachers' lounge. Soon Principal MacFalone entered and quieted us down. "I won't take much of your time," he said, "but I wanted to point out that our great staff here has only gotten better with the addition of the rookie this year." All eyes turned toward me, the "rookie."

I felt a rush of pride as he continued, "I sat in his Math for Daily Living class this morning and witnessed something truly remarkable. I know that class can be tough to teach, but somehow the rookie had them engaged and eager to learn. Kids were raising their hands and answering questions— it was amazing! In your free time, I suggest you exchange ideas with the rookie so our great team can get even better!"

It was a proud moment for me. More importantly, I couldn't wait to tell the students about the great report. I could have accepted the normal expectations for classroom evaluations, but I had no interest in being normal. I flipped the narrative from being about me to making those kids look great. As a result, I got more out of each of those students—*just like I want to get the most out of you.*

To do that, let's start by flipping the narrative on four dream-killing beliefs that hold people back.

BELIEF #1: I HAVE NO TIME.

Sure, Mark, I'd love to do more, you might be thinking, *if only I had the time to do it. But I already feel like I'm maxing out every minute and just have nothing left to give.* I hear you. As our family grew to three children while I was teaching, we had more bills than cash. My basketball coaching brought in a little extra money, but we never got ahead.

Then my father invited me to start a side hustle with a telecommunications company. Back then, it wasn't uncommon for people to pay a lot of money per minute for long-distance phone service. (Yes, those were the days when some people still used those rotary phones you see in old movies!) This company offered a dramatically less expensive way to make those long-distance calls. Plus, it offered a direct-selling business opportunity where we could have the freedom and flexibility to be in charge of our own success. You might think of direct sales as social selling, a cutting-edge industry that rewards people who introduce others to helpful products or services. However, even after my dad convinced us to join him, I didn't really do anything with it for several months for one very simple reason: I believed I had no time.

I could see the opportunity to grow our own direct-selling business with that company, but I couldn't see how we could fit one more thing into our already overflowing schedule. Cindy was already running a small day care in our home and cleaning houses to help us make ends meet. However, we finally realized that if we wanted different results, we had to try something different. We agreed to make no excuses and find the time, and we made the commitment to work on the business opportunity one night a week.

My wife knew I was serious about this business and my dreams when I gave up my one night of playing sports. I knew that if I reinvested that time into my dream, I would eventually have plenty of time to do more of what I loved. It sounds counterintuitive, but I realized I did, in fact, have time in the long term *if* I was willing to sacrifice in the short term. Think about things you do—scroll on your phone, watch Netflix, just being everything to everyone—whatever it is, you have time.

Then something amazing happened. Our business began to experience some success. Before long, we actually had more cash than bills. It was time to celebrate! But then I thought, *What else might be possible for us?* When we worked our Dream

Muscles even more and committed to two nights a week, the business soared.

What could you do to create more time for you to pursue your dreams? Wake up earlier? Find a more flexible job? Listen to podcasts and learn while you drive? Schedule what matters to you first, and then let everything else fill in around it? Set aside one night a week like I did? You don't always need a large chunk of time either. You can use twenty minutes on your lunch break to move your dream forward in some way.

Don't get me wrong—the time crunch feels real when you are stuck in the Dependence Dilemma. It can be tough to think of doing "one more thing." Maybe your current career path gives you the money you need, but it requires most of your time to get it done. At some point, you thought it would give you the freedom and resources to do what you really want to do, but it just hasn't worked out that way. Add your spouse or significant other, children and family, church or community, and some semblance of a social life, and—before you know it—you feel like you're out of time.

At least that's what "normal" tells you. But you can flip the narrative on "normal" by realizing this truth: We always find time for what really matters to us. What if I said I'd give you a brand-new G-Wagon if you'd be willing to work an extra three hours a week? Do you think you'd find the time then? Probably. The question is not, *Do you have time to go after your dreams?* but, *What really matters to you?*

BELIEF #2: I HAVE NO MONEY.

Believe me, when the engine failed on my truck, I was frustrated because I knew we had no money easily available to fix it. So let's just be clear: Money matters. Don't let anyone tell you differently. As Zig Ziglar said, "Money isn't everything, but it ranks right up there with oxygen on the 'got to have it' scale."

When money is scarce, you may feel like you need to do something totally radical—but radical feels impossible when you're stuck. So you stay put and grow a little more frustrated every day. But you can choose to flip that narrative in the same way we just flipped the narrative of not having enough time. Remember that as you put in the dream reps, thinking differently will become your new norm.

You might say you don't have a hundred dollars to invest in a new business opportunity that could change your life. But if I offered you the house of your dreams for only $300, I guarantee you would find a way to make it happen. Why? When you value something highly enough, you will always find the money for it.

Once you flip the narrative, you realize there are a lot of different ways to get the money. When I was a teacher, I lined athletic fields to make extra cash. Even before we started the direct-selling business I've mentioned, we used the little extra money I made on the side to invest in flipping houses before that was cool. Then, even though we could easily have believed we didn't have any money, we found a way to make what we needed for the starter kit for that new business. Because we valued the chance to finally find financial freedom and chase our dreams, we found a way to get the money we needed to make it happen.

And the same is true for you. You could drive for a ride-sharing service or deliver food or packages to make extra money. You could sell collectibles online or pick up some freelance gigs. You might find a part-time job lining sports fields like I did. You could also ask friends or family members to invest in your dreams. The truth is, it has never been easier to get the money you need to pursue what matters to you.

BELIEF #3: I HAVE NO OPPORTUNITIES.

It might feel like there could never be anything different than what you're doing right now, but here is one thing I've learned: Opportunities tend to present themselves when you expect to find them. If you don't expect to see them, you won't.

I grabbed whatever side gig opportunities I could find to make extra money, such as running basketball camps. I'm not saying I enjoyed every experience, but I learned from each of them and leaned in to a new dream. I kept the momentum going with small real-estate deals on the side. Eventually, as I learned and grew, real estate helped me fund my other dreams. The question is this: If you don't see any opportunities right now, what opportunities are you expecting to see?

You may have tried different opportunities before, and they didn't work out. Maybe you remember a time you dared to dream in the past and were disappointed, or you hear that nagging voice inside your head saying, *Everyone is lucky but you.* A lot of people think that dreams only come true for everyone else. However, I knew that if I refused to quit, I would greatly increase my odds of success because it's hard to beat a person who never gives up.

What if you flipped the narrative and saw those previous attempts as stepping stones? You tried. You learned. And that's okay. Again, your new norm is to think differently than what the rest of the world tells you.

You may need to try a number of different things to discover your best path because success seldom happens in a straight line. You'll have ups and downs and all sorts of changes in direction along the way. Just keep working your Dream Muscle and keep moving forward. What if instead of resigning yourself to saying *no*, you conditioned yourself to say *yes?* Even if an opportunity feels small to you, let that yes be a stepping stone to set you up for your next dream.

In fact, a secret I've learned is that the greatest opportunities are easily missed because they're disguised as ordinary, day-to-day life. Start thinking of the side gig you took on to make a little extra money as a stepping stone toward something else. But what if it were something more? You might not realize it at the moment, but what if that stepping stone *is* the opportunity you've been longing for? For my wife and me, we initially saw the direct-selling opportunity as a way to get more cash than bills. That was it. But that side gig turned out to be the one that changed everything once we focused on making it happen.

The truth is that when we signed up with our first direct-selling company, we let the starter kit sit for months after we invested in it. Day after day went by with us thinking we had no time and no opportunities—but opportunity was sitting on the shelf right in front of us the entire time.

Pause for a minute to ask yourself a question. I want to challenge you to dig deep to give yourself an honest answer: *What opportunities are "sitting on the shelf" in front of you right now?* Don't just pass over that question. Put this book down for a few minutes if you have to and truly listen to what is stirring within you.

We usually know when we have to try something different. And it may feel awkward or uncomfortable to try something unfamiliar, so open your eyes to the opportunities you already have. Choose to say *yes.*

BELIEF #4: I NEED TO PLAY IT SAFE.

People are often scared of doing the wrong thing when what they should be scared of is doing nothing. Don't let that be you. *Think differently.*

The appearance of security keeps too many people from following their dreams. After two years of building our new business opportunity, we were making enough money to replace my teaching salary. But Cindy and I had three kids, and I knew health-care benefits were necessary for our family. So I stayed put for a little longer, afraid to fully focus on my dreams. Of course, healthcare is important, but staying in a job you don't like isn't the only way to take care of your health needs. You can find ways to make a little more money and buy your own insurance instead of letting it be an excuse to stay put and stay miserable.

You also need to flip the narrative about that word *safe*. The truth is that nothing is ever as "safe" or "stable" as you might think. At any point, the company you work for could downsize and let you go. Or the bosses could tighten the budget and cut back on the benefits that were keeping you there in the first place. Figure out what health insurance costs, and then don't let that number hold you back a second longer. Don't let a few hundred dollars a month stop you from giving yourself permission to follow your dreams.

You may need to get real with the numbers—and I'm not just saying that as a former math teacher. When we created a budget to figure out what we would need to make in order for me to leave teaching, we looked at how much was coming out of every paycheck for things such as insurance and retirement. We added in employer contributions and found out what they were really costing us. That gave us actual data we could use to know what we needed to earn to make our dreams come true. We didn't just wing it. Knowing our numbers made it more likely we would succeed.

So, what are your numbers? How much are your fears actually costing you? You may be surprised to learn that you're staying stuck for a lot less than you think. Even worse, you might be paying more to avoid your dream than what you would happily pay to achieve it.

What has playing it safe gotten you so far? If you sense a stirring within, you clearly want more. So the question is this: What will you do about it? Do you just want to settle for more of the same? I hope not. Don't wait for the perfect opportunity. Just start.

If any of these excuses have been holding you back, don't panic. Remember, it's normal to feel stuck. But you don't have to accept the way things are just because that's the way they've always been. You don't have to settle for being stuck. You simply must be willing to believe that something better is possible.

If you don't believe anything better really is possible for you, I have great news: It doesn't matter. You can begin *before* you believe.

BORROW MY BELIEF

I began before I believed, and you can too. Once you start dreaming again, you'll start taking action. Then, as you take action, your belief levels will naturally rise. You don't have to be fully convinced it is possible to break free from the Dependence Dilemma to engage the Dream Phenomenon. You just need to start, and your beliefs will follow.

Before I walk you step-by-step through the Dream Phenomenon that fueled our success, I want to point out that some people may have already found a life or career path doing what they truly love to do. Their work fulfills their needs and truly aligns with their dreams—and that's great. There's nothing wrong with that. If that's you and you're already living your dream life, then the rest of this book will help you take your current dream to *a whole 'notha level.*

However, if you struggle to believe freedom is possible, just do this: *Borrow my belief.* That's right. Borrow the belief I have in you as you need it. Because I believe you were born to dream! I believe that if you start using your Dream Muscle and following the Dream Phenomenon—the exact process I followed— you *will* free yourself from being stuck between that rock and hard place. You *will* enjoy greater freedom that will bless you and those you care about every day in every way. As you do, I promise that you— and the rest of the world—will be amazed at what happens next.

Unfortunately, not everyone will take me up on my offer to borrow my belief. I know some people will choose to close this book and return to day-to-day survival mode. When I started my new business while I was still teaching, some of the teachers at the school saw the opportunity and joined me. But only a few stuck with it. The fact that you picked up this book and are tracking with me makes me think you're one of us dreamers. You're ready to believe. You've given yourself permission to dream. I'm so excited for you! It's going to be an incredible journey together, and I'm eager to coach you one-on-one throughout this book as you take each step in the Dream Phenomenon.

Just remember: Success seldom happens in a straight line. You have no idea where this dream journey can take you, so buckle up! I know it will be an adventure because my own journey started when we just wanted more cash than bills and grew to making enough money to leave my teaching job behind. It started with flipping houses, and it grew to owning our own tropical island paradise. It started with launching a new health company, and it grew to becoming one of the top companies in the industry with over $700 million in annual sales. It started with loving cowboy stories, and it grew to owning a ten-thousand-acre cattle ranch that was the location to film a Western movie. And now I'm getting calls to produce more movies! It started with my desire to share the Dream Phenomenon that I used to succeed, and it turned into this bestselling book. (Wait . . . I'm getting ahead of myself. But that's the dream!)

If you would have told me that any of those things were possible back when I felt stuck, I would have told you that you were crazy. But here we are. From teacher and coach to millionaire to billionaire. You just never know where your dream journey will take you, but I promise you this: Crazy is contagious.

So if you're ready to become a professional dreamer, just borrow my belief and give yourself permission to dream. If you're ready to break free from the Dependence Dilemma and leave those excuses behind, join me on this journey. And if you're ready to finally live the life of your dreams, let's experience the Dream Phenomenon together.

It's gonna be a wild ride!

YOUR DREAM PLAN

1. **Determine your Dream Muscle fitness.** When was the last time you allowed yourself to dream? Has it been a while since you worked out your Dream Muscle? Take a moment now to engage in your first workout by asking yourself these questions:

   What will be the first dream I want to pursue?

   Why does my dream feel meaningful to me?

2. **Find your new normal.** It's time to *think differently* and flip the narrative. Which of the four excuses sounds most familiar to you? No time? No money? No opportunities? A need to feel safe?

   Finish this sentence: *I'm afraid that if I follow my dreams . . .*

How might you reframe that narrative into a belief that stirs you to dream more?

3. **Connect with your future self.** Imagine you are living the life of your dreams in the future. Write a letter from your future self to your present self.

   How does it feel to be living your dreams? What dreams have you achieved? What do your days look like? Do you have more time to pursue what matters to you? Who is with you? How happy are you? Free your imagination to be as detailed as possible.

   Most importantly, what encouragement would your future self give you to fight for the dreams you have today?

   Put your letter in an envelope and keep it close to you. Read it often to remind yourself that you have given yourself permission to dream.

Get in the Game

*The day you start dreaming is
the day you start living.*

Are you still buckled in? You might want to brace yourself. I'm about to tell you my secret to achieving such incredible success. Right here. Right now.

Once you hear it, everything will change for you. Are you ready?

Here it is: *I got in the game.*

What, Mark? That's it?

Yep. That's it—or at least that's where it all starts.

To borrow from my basketball coaching experience, if you're letting excuses keep you from taking action, you're not out on the court. You're just sitting in the stands watching other people go after a life of more. That's why it's the first step in the Dream Phenomenon. Nothing else is possible until you get in the game.

To tell you the truth, there were many times when I was still teaching that I felt like I had one foot on the court and the other in the stands. There were many times I thought I was in the game, but it was like I couldn't bring myself to go *all in*. I was hungry. I was looking for opportunities, but I hesitated and bounced back and forth between being an Active Dreamer and an Inactive Dreamer. I let my excuses—having no time, money, or opportunities and wanting to play it safe—keep me stuck in the stands.

Then I found my Get-in-the-Game Moment. It happened a few months after we made the decision to join my dad in that telecommunications business opportunity. We paid the money and got our starter-kit box. Then we put it on the shelf while we hoped for other opportunities.

Finally, after watching us continue to struggle, my dad asked me when I was going to act on the opportunity. I tried to tell him we just didn't have time, but he said words I will never forget: "Mark, if you keep doing what you're doing, you're still going to have the same challenges in ten years that you have now. You'll be telling me the same excuses and you'll still be feeling stuck—only you'll be ten years older because you didn't do anything about it."

That hurt, but Dad was right. That's when I realized the truth: *I wasn't even in the game.* But how could I *not* have been? After all, I was doing everything I was supposed to do. I had gone to college, gotten my degree, and was giving everything I had to my career. Plus, I was hungry for more and trying new things—at least some of the time. And yet I kept pushing aside that stirring within until the moment I realized a startling truth: By waiting for

HUDDLE UP!

As we journey together, I'll call us to Huddle Up! to share a tip, ask questions, or inspire you to action. Whenever I talk to groups or give a speech, I end in a huddle because huddles let you see who is in the game with you. You can tell if someone is connecting with you or is looking up into the stands. So when you see Huddle Up! pause and let's connect.

Let's start with some questions about what might be stirring within you. Ask yourself: *Am I in the stands watching other people live their dreams? Even worse, am I living only to help someone else build a dream life instead of my own? Am I ready to lace up my shoes and get out on the court?*

I hope you're ready because *you* need *you* in the game!

the "perfect" opportunity, I had taken myself out of the game. But when I took that starter kit off the shelf, I got out of the stands and onto the court of life and said, "Let's go!"

My Get-in-the-Game Moment came when Dad called me to step out on to the court and I said yes. If you've never had someone do the same for you, let me be the first. If you sense that stirring within, *now* is the time to get in the game and say *yes* to your dreams. You can stay in the Dependence Dilemma and keep doing the best you can, but then what will be different for you in ten years? You'll still have the same challenges, but you'll be ten years older and still giving the same excuses.

I answered the call and took action. Now it's time for *your* Get-in-the-Game Moment because the day you start dreaming is the day you start living.

THE DREAMLINE

People dream on a sliding scale of passion and possibility. I call it the Dreamline. The more passionate you are about your dream and the more you believe it is possible to achieve it, the more active your Dream Muscle becomes.

When passion and possibility are low, you're in the Inactive Zone. When passion and possibility increase, you move into the Active Zone on the Dreamline.

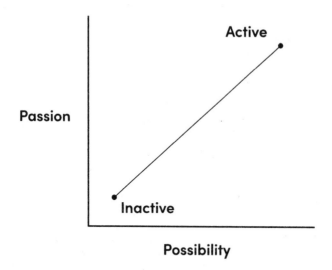

There are two things to know about the Dreamline. First, everyone is on it because everyone is born to dream. Even if you know someone who claims they've never dreamed before, trust me, that person is on it, even if their dreams appear undetectable.

Second, your location on the Dreamline is not fixed. You can move from Inactive toward Active at whatever pace you choose. Feeling stuck today doesn't mean you need to feel stuck tomorrow. When you give yourself permission to get in the game, you can move quickly up the Dreamline.

Now, let me give you a caution: The scale slides both ways. Even if you are an Active Dreamer, if you stop using your Dream Muscle, you can slide right back down into the Inactive Zone. When it comes to your ability to dream, if you don't use it, you'll lose it. There have certainly been times in my life when I've been less active than others, and there have been times when I've felt like a yo-yo on a string moving up and down the Dreamline. Fortunately, I've chosen to hang out on the Active end of the Dreamline, and that has made all the difference.

So where are you right now? How actively are you dreaming? You can find out where you are on the Dreamline by using a simple tool I call the Dream Detector.

The Dream Detector

Indicate how frequently the following statements are true for you to reveal what sort of dreamer you are right now. Give yourself points for each answer based on the following scale:

1 point—Never
2 points—Rarely
3 points—Sometimes
4 points—Often
5 points—Always

1. I give myself permission to dream *big* every day.

2. I pursue what matters to me instead of what I feel pressured to do.
3. I plan time to dream on a regular basis.
4. I believe I was born to dream.
5. I believe I can take action to change my life for the better.
6. I believe I have all the time, energy, and creativity I need to pursue my dream.
7. I write down my dreams and review them regularly.
8. I say my dreams out loud.
9. I use pictures and images to help me clearly visualize my dreams.
10. I minimize negative voices and surround myself with people who believe in me.
11. I spend time with people who encourage me to pursue my dreams.
12. I seek out and spend time with mentors who have done what I dream to do.
13. I step out before I know how it will turn out.
14. I let go of the perception of safety and security to discover something better for me and those I care about.
15. I would rather try and fail than fail without ever trying.

16. I believe learning from mistakes is the only path to success.
17. I know I can find a way to overcome, even if I encounter a setback.
18. I am okay with being uncomfortable for a while to achieve my dreams.
19. When I achieve any success in life, I make sure to celebrate it.
20. Once I achieve a dream, I start imagining a new and greater dream.

Now add up your score to see which type of Dreamer you are: _____

20–35: Inactive Dreamer
36–56: Passive Dreamer
57–72: Aspiring Dreamer
73–89: Active Dreamer
90–100: Phenomenal Dreamer!

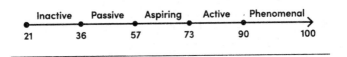

How did you do? The good news is that you can improve your score. No matter your current dream level, you can choose to move toward becoming a more Active Dreamer by following the Dream Phenomenon process. You could even become a Phenomenal Dreamer who lives and acts as if their impossible is possible.

It's my goal to coach and equip you to become that Phenomenal Dreamer, but the first step is to Get in the Game. Start where you are and work your Dream Muscle to prepare to take your dreams to *a whole 'notha level.*

YOUR DREAM FINDER

Great, Mark, you might be thinking. *Thanks for helping me see I need to get in the game, but I'm not sure what dream to pursue.*

Not a problem. Let's keep it super simple: *Choose to pursue what matters to you.*

This means there isn't necessarily a right dream or a wrong dream for you. So let's ask some practical questions to help you reengage with what lights you up.

1. **What energizes you?** Pay attention to what energizes you because your dream follows your energy. If *you* aren't energetic about what you pursue, you won't be able to sustain the effort needed to get you there.

Do you know what energizes you, or do you simply run on autopilot every day, doing the same things again and again without much thought? Do you go from coffee to kids to work—or whatever your morning routine might be—without really being aware of how you feel about what you do?

In my experience, most people are often not fully present in the moments of life or aware enough to find out what energizes them. But you don't have to be that way. In fact, it's not that hard to do. Simply tune in, take inventory of where you spend your time, and ask yourself how it feels. Notice those times when you feel especially energized and enthusiastic. But also note any times when you feel drained or depleted.

How do you feel when you are with family or friends? How did you feel in that work meeting yesterday? How does that side gig you just started make you feel? Those energy indicators are all trying to tell you something because there are things you are naturally wired to enjoy more than others in different seasons of life. When you discover what those are, you can narrow your focus and empower yourself to dream.

You may need to revisit this every year to tune in to what energizes you now. Because what used to energize you before may not now. For many years, I was energized by the thought of being a head basketball coach. But then, after years of doing it, it shocked me to realize it wasn't filling me up anymore. Though I used to play basketball all the time, now I'm really energized by pickleball. Things change.

It's easy to put your life on autopilot because you used to love doing something. But by paying attention to what energizes you now, you may realize it simply doesn't fill you up anymore. I want you to try something: When you're in your next meeting, connecting with a friend, or doing focused work, pause to consider if the activity drains you or give you energy. That's a good starting point to begin to see where your dreams are pointing.

2. **What are you good at?** Over the years, I've had hundreds of thousands of people on my payroll, and what I've seen is that many people don't even know what they're good at.

That's unfortunate because everyone is talented at something.

Every person naturally does something better than most people. For some, it might be speaking or communicating. For others, it might be thinking or creating. It may be something as simple and as powerful as making people feel welcome. Another person may be a YouTuber who easily masters storytelling via video editing and production. For others, running a business may hit the sweet spot. Whatever it may be for you, I guarantee you are really good at some things, even if you're not so sure you are.

Think back to those times when people seemed impressed by something you did. Even if it seemed like a small thing to you, when have other people told you that you were good at something? Did those skills seem to come easily for you whereas other people said they struggled? It's easy to see stronger skills in others, but what are those strong skills for you?

Give yourself the opportunity to try new things to discover what you're good at. What you discover may surprise you. When I was a teacher and coach in school, I had no idea that I would also be good at being a teacher and coach in business. Likewise, after being married for more than forty years, my wife, Cindy, surprised me by deciding to try her hand at painting— and she's really good! So don't just assume you already know what you're good at. Try some different things. Your hunger to learn something new may be an opportunity to discover more about yourself.

Make it a habit to watch for these things you are good at. As people point them out or you notice that you naturally perform at a higher level than others, make a note of it. Often our dreams lie at the center of that place where our energy, skills, and a third element come together.

3. **Where is the need?** I believe you were given the seeds of your dreams for a reason. Dreams are not just about making ourselves happy or having fun with those we love. Don't get me wrong—I love what I do every day. I love doing all of it with the people I care about. But if I meet no greater need than fulfilling my own happiness, I know I will feel unfulfilled. Because in the end, it's not all about me. I believe I've been given these dreams to help make the world a better place.

What is the need that your unique energy and skills can meet? Maybe your heart is drawn toward helping people who struggle with a particular challenge. Perhaps there is a cause that deeply moves you that needs a podcasting voice to shine a light on it. Or maybe hurting people can be helped by your creativity and care. I'm passionate about helping people who feel stuck and are not dreaming to their fullest potential, but your story will likely be different.

Often people find the need they are called to when they pursue what energizes them and put their talents to work. Just by getting in the game, they discover clarity and a greater sense of purpose as they go. My daughter Kindsey was energized by helping others eat healthy before any of that was cool. She created a cookbook for people to use and started engaging with them. As she did, she discovered people often didn't have time to cook healthy meals. So she began to provide meal prep services to coach people on healthy eating habits and show them the benefits of healthy eating. She set out in one direction but discovered a different need as she put her talents to work.

Be prepared that what you discover may surprise you. Remember, we dreamers see things differently than the "normal" world around us. We can change entire industries by seeing opportunities where no one else does. So don't restrict yourself to thinking about the need in the same way everyone else has always done. *Be willing to be bold and to redefine "normal."*

One person I know discovered an unconventional need: couples wanted to have their favorite dogs with them on their wedding day. She created a service to care for the dogs throughout the big day and then bring them to the couple for special intentional interactions. As a result, the couple gets to see their dogs without disrupting their busy wedding day plans.

Another example is that of entrepreneur John Henry, who saw many people struggling to move forward in life because they didn't have fair access to credit using the traditional credit score system. He used his insurance expertise and passion for social justice to create a gamified app that lets people qualify for credit based on their driving records.

So, what needs are you uniquely qualified to fulfill? How can you make the world a better place by applying your energy and talents? The needs are limited only by our ability to dream of new solutions.

You don't have to have all the answers right away. In fact, it may take time for the answers to become completely clear for you. And that's okay.

THE WINNING PLAY

Just because you get in the game doesn't mean you'll always call the right plays. Sometimes you need to run a few to find what works best for you.

I know how scary it can feel to finally get in the game and step out on the court. I also know how frustrating it can be not to win your first time—or even your second or third. Each side hustle I tried when I was still teaching helped move us forward, but none of them brought in enough extra money for me to quit my day job. Those first plays gave us a little extra cash to try the next thing and prepared us to say yes when my dad challenged us to step up.

When we were just looking to make more cash than bills, I read a book written by Robert Kiyosaki called *Rich Dad Poor Dad*. That book opened my mind and made me realize I didn't want to be an employee for the rest of my life. It created a hunger in me to know what an entrepreneur is and to learn how to create income without trading time for dollars. Real estate was a key part of my plan to create more cash flow through passive income.

Have you ever watched those home renovation shows where someone buys an old home and tries to modernize it? Well, that's what Cindy and I did as one of our early plays. We bought houses that needed a little work, fixed them up, then either sold them for a profit or rented them to cover our mortgage costs and then some.

The profits we made off those houses allowed us to pay off some credit cards. That was huge for us! We celebrated as we felt some of that pressure between the rock and the hard place begin to lessen. *Maybe this is the vehicle we need,* we thought, *to get the freedom we want.* We did this a few more times until we had acquired several rental properties.

At first, we thought individual rental properties would earn us enough extra money to get the freedom we wanted. However, after renting the houses for a few years, we found that we just didn't like running all over town being landlords. We loved real estate as an investing path, but the way we were going about it then didn't give us the flexibility we wanted.

So we sold the houses and bought a twelve-unit apartment building with an indoor pool. Instead of driving all over town to collect rent or do maintenance, we had twelve units all in one place. I've got to tell you, at that point I thought we had arrived and that we'd be set for life. However, the truth is that repairing stuff was never my gift. I ended up thinking that if I never had to unclog another toilet, I would live a very happy life! So I realized my next dream was to be able to afford plumbers and electricians. And as much as I enjoyed using the pool with my family, it also turned out to be a bigger maintenance headache than we expected.

Right around that time, I had my Get-in-the-Game Moment with my dad. When we finally opened that direct-selling starter kit, we realized the business had the potential for us to make more money faster than real estate alone. And after a few months, it started taking off.

While we initially thought we might be able to use real estate to break free from the Dependence Dilemma, the direct-selling business opportunity turned out to be the main piece of the winning play for us. The new business gave us more money to invest back into real estate, something I still love to do today.

Fast-forward a couple of years. We ended up moving from the small town of Allegan, Michigan, to the larger city of Grand Rapids. Ready to use the money we had made in our business, we decided we weren't done expanding our real estate dreams. We began exploring the idea of commercial properties and renting offices to businesses, which would eliminate the things we didn't like about renting apartments.

With the money we made from our direct-selling efforts, we bought our first commercial building with more than a dozen office suites to rent. The very first thing we did? Hire an incredible maintenance guy. No more midnight calls about clogged toilets.

It worked so well for us that we bought two more buildings and ended up renting out almost forty office suites. While we didn't end up retiring as commercial real estate magnates in Michigan, we did continue renting offices for many years. Eventually, real estate gave us the money we needed to start another business—the one that would fuel our breakthrough success.

That's not to say it was easy. Being in the game always demands a lot of work, but it wasn't until we had reactivated our Dream Muscle that we realized how close we had been to giving up dreaming altogether.

I share our journey with you because I want you to know that once you get on the court, you may have to run a few different plays to find the ones that win for you. It's a step-by-step process. Just because something didn't work like you thought it would the first time doesn't mean you should get off the court. It may mean you need to pivot, learn, and try another play. Each time you try something new, your Dream Muscle grows and you get that much closer to your dream.

You may need to make a few moves once you get in the game to pursue what matters to you, but it will be worth it. If I were you, doing it all over again, I would encourage you to pursue what matters to you and use the initial money you make to give yourself margin so you can lean in to your dreams.

Maybe you've tried a side hustle before. Perhaps you started a blog, social media channel, or e-commerce store. Maybe you turned your house, apartment, or spare bedroom into a short-term rental, or delivered food to people's doors to make an extra buck. Maybe you had started studying for a license, degree, or certificate, but then something came up and it all just fell to the wayside. As a result, you left the court and went back up into the stands.

I get it. When you work your Dream Muscle without seeing the results you want at first, it can be hard to keep dreaming and trying new things. You may start to feel

> **HUDDLE UP!**
>
> One way to make the most of any extra money you earn via side hustles is to reinvest it into similar opportunities that can make you even more money. If you make some money with a rideshare service, consider using it to get certified to do freelance work or to advertise for your other business ventures. Use your profits to reinvest in you!

like you're letting your people down and not living up to your full potential. When that happens and the disbelief kicks in, it can be so easy to tell yourself, *This is never going to happen for me.* That is when you are in the greatest danger of stopping dreaming altogether.

But now you know you're not alone, and this is not the end of your story. Because you—and only you—can act to achieve your dreams. This is your time. This is *your* Get-in-the-Game Moment. Today is the day you choose to leave the stands and turn the Dream Phenomenon loose in your life.

You may not have intentionally created the life you are living now. You may not even have made a conscious decision to stay in the stands. But starting today, you can choose to reactivate your Dream Muscle, step out onto the court, and get back in the game.

You don't need to wait for "one day." This is Day One for you. Are you ready to play? *Then let's go!*

YOUR DREAM PLAN

1. **Your Dream Detector.** We are all born to dream, but to move forward, you need to know where you are on the Dreamline right now. If you skipped the Dream Detector tool as you read, go back and use it now to discover if you are an Inactive, Passive, Aspiring, Active, or Phenomenal Dreamer.

    Record your current Dream Detector score:

    Right now, I am a(n) _____ Dreamer.

2. **Answer this question as honestly as you possibly can:** If there were no limits or restrictions, what would you want to do, pursue, be, have, experience, and enjoy?

3. **Energy.** If you're ready to get in the game but still aren't sure what to dream about, make an inventory of your feelings as you go about life. Pay attention to how you feel while you're doing your work or are in your meetings and interactions. Then reflect on what you feel:

    What invigorated you? Why?

What drained your energy? Why?

4. **Talents:** To help clarify what you are good at, fill in the blanks for the following thought-starter statements:

- I am naturally good at _____ _____.

- I've been told I can _____ _____ better than most.

- I've learned to _____ _____ exceptionally well.

- It was easy for me to figure out how to _____.

- Other people always ask my help to _____.

- People struggle with _____ _____, but I think it's easy.

- I'm proud to say that I know I am good at _____.

Now, take it to the next level by turning these statements into affirmations of the unique value you bring to the world.

5. **Needs:** When you think about what energizes you, are there certain problems in the world that you're passionate about helping to solve? Are there needs that you have a hunger to meet even if you don't see the path to doing so right now? List some of them here:

Think about those needs in the context of your own circle of influence. Where do you see opportunities in front of you right now?

Where do you see potential opportunities you might pursue in the future as your Dream Muscle grows?

Say It and See It

If you can say it and see it, you can achieve it.

Have you ever had a time in your life when you felt excited just to be alive? Starting our first direct-selling company was that kind of time for me. A whole new world had opened up, full of possibilities that seemed to grow every day.

I was still teaching, of course, but I could finally be my own boss to some extent. Plus, I had started getting paid based on my own work ethic rather than being limited to a 3 percent annual increase within "the system." I was still waking up to an alarm clock, but now I found myself eager to jump out of bed, ready to act on my dreams.

Only a few months after we'd started our one-night-a-week commitment to grow our business, Cindy and I achieved our first dream of having more cash than bills. It felt amazing, and achieving that first dream gave us a taste of what we could expect if we kept going. Now that our Dream Muscles were active and ready for more, we needed to get clear on exactly what "more" meant for us. We needed step 2 of the Dream Phenomenon: Say It and See It.

With that first dream checked off our list, we flew to Dallas, Texas, to attend a convention the telecommunications company hosted every year. To be honest, we hadn't flown more than a handful of times in our entire lives or even taken a vacation without the kids, so the travel was half the fun. Plus, this was the first time we would get to meet the other salespeople and managers in person.

We still didn't quite know what we were getting ourselves into and half joked that we wanted to make sure it wasn't some kind of cult. In fact, we were some of the first people in Michigan to work with this company.

When we arrived in Dallas, we drove to the Omni Hotel and made our way into a huge convention room where we saw hundreds of people like us. They were all full of energy and passion as they milled about, catching up like they'd been friends for years.

Since we didn't know anyone else, we just wanted to slip into the back of the spacious room and observe.

The event started with a few great motivational speakers. I hadn't seen anything like this before, but they sure knew how to pump up and inspire a crowd. Cindy and I could just feel the buzz of excitement around us from everyone in the room. They all seemed genuinely glad to be there. And I could feel the hope of possibility growing within me too.

After the speakers finished, the company leaders came onstage to present awards for highest sales. As they handed out the awards, they said a few words about the winners—their names, backgrounds, and achievements. Soon they were handing out checks. And the checks just kept getting bigger and bigger!

Then they invited someone onstage who really got my attention. They introduced him as a former high school basketball coach—just like me. And a former teacher—just like me. He seemed to be a pretty normal-looking guy from Kentucky—until they announced the reason he was there. He was making $10,000 a month. *Whoa!* That got my attention. What stood out most was one word they used to describe him: *former* coach and teacher.

I felt like I'd been hit by lightning. My eyes got a little wider as I stepped away from the wall and excitedly turned to Cindy. "He was a coach and teacher just like me, and now he's getting an award for having made $10,000 a month," I told her. "I didn't know that was possible! Cindy, that could be us!" I imagine I felt a lot like people who had been told no one could ever run a four-minute mile. Then someone did it, and suddenly all sorts of people were doing it.

For the first time, I started to believe Cindy and I could radically change our lives. Even though we were always dreamers, I'd say we had been hovering in Passive Dreamer status. We'd begun making more cash than bills, and we did so more easily than we had thought possible. But seeing that former coach and teacher earn $10,000 a month—that was an aha! moment that moved us up the Dreamline. That night, we became Aspiring Dreamers. I started imagining game-changing dreams. If we could hit $10,000 a

HUDDLE UP!

Now that you've had a chance to think about your dream and have given yourself permission to pursue it, ask yourself, *Is there someone in the world who's already achieved something similar?* Then Google it. I suspect you'll find someone who inspires you the way that former coach and teacher inspired us. Maybe follow someone on Instagram or YouTube, and see how they did it. Let that person's story inspire you!

month, maybe I could become a *former* teacher too. I could have a lot more flexibility and never have to wake up to the sound of an alarm clock again. I could spend a lot more time with my kids whenever I wanted to. My head was spinning with possibilities!

After the event, we found the *former* coach and teacher and introduced ourselves to him and his wife. They seemed like perfectly normal people, which further instilled our belief that we could do what he had done.

We couldn't wait to get back to our hotel room and start planning. We had finally seen what was possible and understood what we had to do next. I wasn't ready to leave teaching, but I could clearly see it was time to take our opportunity to *a whole 'notha level*. And that's exactly what we did.

THE POWER OF POSSIBILITY

The lesson I learned after that day was this: *If you can say it and see it, you can achieve it.* When we saw people like us succeeding at what we wanted to do, we knew we could also do it. When we returned to Allegan, our clear vision of seeing ourselves walk across the stage drove us forward. Seeing it done by others supercharged our belief levels and fueled our work ethic. We started working even more nights on the business. Soon, our monthly earnings became a drop in the bucket on the way to our new dream of earning $10,000 a month.

As humans, we seem to struggle to do what we can't already see being done. I already knew the power of visualization from working with athletes for so many years. As part of their training, many professional athletes visualize themselves successfully following through on their golf swing or making their basketball shot. They know if they cannot see success happening in their own minds, it is a lot less likely to happen in reality. But if they can see it, it's as if the human mind has a road map to follow to find a way to make it happen.[7]

What you do is also influenced by what you say. If you say you're going to do something, you're more likely to follow through on it. But what you say is controlled by what you think. It all ties back to the idea that if you envision yourself doing something, you plant the possibility in your own mind that you actually can do it.

If you can imagine yourself living as if your dream has already become reality, your mind becomes more focused. The human brain doesn't make a significant distinction between your current and future reality. At the most basic level, if you see it as real, you will act as if it is real. Those belief-informed actions will then produce results that create the reality you want to see. When you condition your brain in this way, you train your subconscious to take the steps needed to achieve your dreams.

When Cindy and I saw that former coach and teacher getting an award for making $10,000 a month, we were able to see ourselves on that stage receiving an award of our own. We started dreaming about earning that much every month. Even though it would take work and time to make that happen, seeing it in our minds and imagining the feel of the paper check in our hands made it seem achievable. We were more motivated than ever to do whatever we needed to do to turn our dream into reality.

In just a few years, our business efforts really took off. We, too, were walking across a stage, getting even-larger checks. And I found myself using this technique to produce success in other areas of my life as well. I realized that sometimes you need to see it, and sometimes all you need to do is say it.

Fast-forward a bit. My journey eventually resulted in our starting a new company called It Works! We initially sold groundbreaking body wraps for tightening and toning. As we followed that dream, Cindy and I decided to host the sales team at our house during the winter for dream-building activities. However, we found that people didn't really want to travel to Michigan in the winter. Go figure! So I began thinking about moving somewhere warmer.

We were still just mulling it over until one evening when I was chatting with my dad.

"Dad, I'm thinking about moving the company to Florida." I sort of blurted it out because I wasn't sure how he would respond. It certainly wasn't normal business procedure to move an entire company across the country.

He sat back and thought about my statement for a minute, and then said, "Why would you move a company that's doing so well in Michigan down to Florida? People don't just move multimillion-dollar companies. And do you really think your team would go with you? Don't they have houses and families and everything? That's a lot to ask of them."

I didn't know the answer to that question, but it started with me stating my dream. After that conversation, I started mentioning the idea of moving to a few members of my leadership team to see what they thought about it. One key leader on the team got so excited that he said he'd drive the bus to Florida! In fact, it seemed that everyone I talked to was ready to pick up and leave. So Cindy and I and the team started looking for the right space. Then one of my team members called me from Florida where, unbeknownst to me, she had gone to scout a location. "Mark, I found a church you'd love," she said excitedly, "and the city is perfect. Let's start packing!"

Over the course of the next two years, we moved the growing company headquarters to Florida. Almost the entire leadership team moved with us. Apparently, it wasn't too difficult after all to convince people to leave the Michigan winters behind.

Looking back now, I realize that saying the dream out loud was more for my own benefit. By putting it out there as a new, possible future reality, I really was giving myself the opportunity to adjust to it.

Now, a word of caution: This principle of Say It and See It works in reverse too. If you speak negative words to yourself, either out loud or in your head, you'll struggle to move past those limiting thoughts. If the future you envision for yourself is clouded by excuses—I have no time, I have no money, I have no opportunities, I need to play it safe—you'll struggle to achieve a bright and hopeful dream. When you can't picture yourself achieving your dream, you subconsciously build a brick wall between you and that dream.

The question is not *if* your words and visuals will shape your dreams but *how* they will do so. The truth is, you are already envisioning a future reality for yourself. For a lot of people, the future reality they envision isn't shaped by their dreams. Instead, their future dreams are forced to fit their current reality. They try to cram their dreams into a predefined—and often negative—space and wonder why nothing seems to work out for them.

Once you give yourself permission to dream again, you can begin the process of shifting your mindset, tearing down and clearing out those excuses. And when you say and see your dreams, you can flip the narrative to create stepping stones that help you reach those dreams.

Say it. See it. Achieve it. It's that simple.

SAY IT OUT LOUD

Mark, do I really have to say it out loud? Of course, I'll never know if you actually say your dream out loud, but I strongly encourage you to do so. A study found that athletes who spoke positive affirmations out loud during competition (yes, where other people could hear them) played better than those who didn't say anything at all.[8] Something about simply expressing your dreams verbally increases your ability to act on them.

I've always had a habit of speaking my dreams out loud. I guess you could say I am a verbal processor. That was one way I thought through how to make them actually happen. I would often say ideas out loud to see how they sounded: "I think I might own a family business someday." Then I might not say anything else for a while as that idea bounced around in my head. Without conscious effort, it would gradually begin to shape my actions.

Saying your dreams out loud, whether to yourself or to another person, holds a lot of power. Although you don't initially say them out loud to get guidance or feedback, you may receive those benefits. Maybe other people's reactions will help clarify things for you, like when I found the leadership team was just as excited about moving to Florida as I was. Or maybe they will help you think through the details of executing your dream. Even if you don't get feedback, putting your thoughts into words creates clarity around your dream and the *why* behind it.

A word of caution here: Be careful *who* you share your dreams with. I've seen many good dreams die after a negative reaction, even a well-meaning one. While you may gain helpful ideas or information from others, this exercise is really more for you to hear yourself speak your dreams than it is for you to seek guidance or feedback from other people on how to execute those dreams.

So, what do I even say? I have a simple process for creating what I call your Dream Script. It all begins with your decision to pursue what matters to you. Remember, you're making the active decision to follow your dream.

The Dream Script has two key parts—your *dream* and your *why.*

First, state your dream. The more specific your dream is, the better. Create a measurable result with actionable steps.[9] If you must start by being vague, go ahead and start there, and work toward greater clarity. But the more details you put into your dream, the more actionable it becomes.

Second, tap into your *why*. As emotional creatures, we're naturally drawn toward the things that tug at our heartstrings and motivate us to pursue our dreams. Think back to the first chapter on claiming permission to dream and really reconnect with your *why*. What is your *why*? Is it to give your family greater financial freedom? To become your own boss? To set a model for your children to follow? To help solve a need you see in the world? Whatever it may be, make it a part of your Dream Script. When you know your why, and repeat it often, you'll be able to more easily push through challenges.

Your Dream Script

I choose to get in the game and pursue my dream of
_____ [your detailed dream] _____
because
_____ [your *why*] _____.

Back when I was working as a teacher, our Dream Script would have been as simple as, "We choose to pursue our dream of earning extra money because we want to have more cash than bills at the end of each month."

Start with what you have now, and get more specific over time. As you build your Dream Muscle, your *why* will get clearer.

Back when I was first learning to use my Dream Muscle, I didn't fully realize the power of my words. Over the years, I've learned to accelerate my dreams by being more intentional about what I say. In addition to moving the company to Florida, I said something else to my dad that sounded crazy at the time: "I'm thinking about buying a golf course in Florida." His arched eyebrows told me I'd gotten his attention.

"Why would you buy a golf course," he asked, "when you could just join a golf club? That would be easier, and you wouldn't have to worry about insurance or upkeep or anything. You could go and play whenever you wanted and just relax."

Those are valid points, I thought, but I kept at it. "I could just join a club, but if I bought one, I could provide more job opportunities. And as the owner, I could host company meetings, retreats, and parties there. No one else in this industry is doing anything like that. We could entertain potential clients, host incredible morale-boosting events, and educate our team like never before. It would give people a destination that's on *a whole 'notha level*, somewhere warm and sunny they could visit instead of snowy Michigan."

"Yeah, you could," Dad admitted. "But who on earth owns a golf course?" I didn't know the answer to that question, but I didn't let it stop me.

Did we do it? Yes. Did it work? You bet it did.

Instead of having to rent facilities somewhere else, we started hosting events at our own golf course. We started small with just thirty people or so. But in just a couple years, we had more than a thousand people attending events there. Not only did it reset the standard for how meetings were done in the industry, it gave us a place where we could go to dream. That golf course proved to be a game changer for us and a catalyst for the rapid growth of our company.

Sometimes, the power of words showed up in the little things I said. When we were still living in the starter home that Cindy and I bought when we first moved to Allegan, I loved reading my collection of classic Western novels by Louis L'Amour. When I did, I would sometimes tell my kids, "I'm going to buy a ranch someday. I'll raise cattle and be a cowboy."

At the time, it seemed a far-fetched dream for a city slicker like me. I wouldn't have blamed them for laughing at their dad for saying it. Nevertheless, I said it, and now I enjoy my hobby of being a cowboy on our own ten-thousand-acre cattle ranch in Florida, the place where we filmed that Western movie I mentioned earlier.

Start where you are right now. You don't have to get your Dream Script perfect. You can always play with the wording and get more concrete as you move forward. Once you get it written down, start every day by saying it out loud. Then, end every day the same way. Making it your first and last thought of the day will sharpen your focus and begin to bring your dream to life.

HUDDLE UP!

Say It and *Share It*. Once you get your Dream Script written, say it out loud. Choose your audience: your spouse, your kids, your parents, your siblings, or your own reflection in the mirror. Or go big and record yourself on video saying your dream out loud so you can share it to your favorite social media accounts. Don't forget to tag #DreamPhenomenon and #MarkPentecost to find support and connect with the Dreamer community!

SEE IT

A young man once had a dream car he wanted to buy. He knew all of the details about it: the make, model, and color he wanted; the type of engine it had; how fast it could go; the best tires for it—literally every detail. So he went down to the dealership and sat in his dream car. He soaked in the feel and smell of the leather seats. He test-drove it around the block several times. Then he took a picture of it.

When he got home, he printed the picture and taped it to the bathroom mirror where he could look at it every morning while he shaved.

His wife saw him drooling over that picture every day and laughed. But he would shake his head and say, "I'm going to do it. I'm going to make the money to buy that car someday."

Then one day, he did just that. He drove that car home and parked it in the driveway.

The very next day, when he got up to shave, he found a new picture on his mirror—of a diamond ring!

I love telling that story because it shows if you can see it, you can achieve it. And you raise the belief level of everyone around you too.

One critical tool we have used at It Works! to see dreams clearly is a Dream Board. The first thing to know about creating a Dream Board is that there isn't any one right way to make one. The idea is straightforward. Put images related to your dream on a board of some sort so you can see a visual reminder of the parts of your dream that most resonate with you.

Some people like to sit down with a stack of magazines and cut out pictures that they glue to a piece of poster board. I was never one for arts and crafts, but when I first introduced this idea to my family, my kids got really excited to talk about their dreams and our family dreams. In fact, now that they're grown and have kids of their own, they've started teaching their own children about dreaming using the same Dream Board concept. No one is too old or too young to see their dreams come to life.

Some people like me are more word-oriented, so writing down our dreams helps bring them to life. Others are more visually oriented and respond better to seeing images of future success. I invite you to give both approaches a try and see what works for you.

If you're not sure where to start with your Dream Board, think back to the exercises from the previous steps. Lean into your *why* and what it is you chose to pursue. Think about your values and what is important to you. If you have paper ready, mark out sections on it for each of those areas. Maybe you make a circle in the top right corner and write "FAMILY" in it so that everything you put in that corner is about your family. Maybe you have another area for career, finances, vacations you want to take, your ideal house, or thoughts about the area in which you want to live someday. Anything and everything can be on this board.

If you can't find pictures to represent your dreams, you can always do what I did and write words down. One of my earliest visualizations of my dreams was just budget numbers scratched on the back of a Big Boy restaurant paper place mat to help me figure out when I could step away from teaching. It doesn't have to be pretty to have great power.

I invite you to grab a magazine, a piece of poster board, a blank sheet of paper—whatever works best for you— and have fun! When you're done, put your Dream Board somewhere where you'll see it every day. Tape it to your bathroom

> **HUDDLE UP!**
>
> Seeing visual representations of your dreams and imagining yourself achieving them creates neural pathways in your brain that help you take the actions necessary to achieve those dreams.[10] Seeing the images of your dreams over and over, day in and day out, creates what neuroscientist Dr. Tara Swart calls "value tagging." Your brain starts to believe these ideas are more important and focuses on them more than others.[11] Seeing becomes believing, which becomes action.

door, hang it on your bedroom wall, or plaster it in the kitchen right above the coffeepot. The point is to look at it every day. If you make boards with your family, consider displaying them all together to show your collective dreams.

I suspect this may be the first of many Dream Boards for you. After you accomplish some of your dreams, you'll want to update your board with the freshest representation of your dreams. We make new Dream Boards every year, and you can do the same.

It's so powerful for me to think that Cindy and I started a dream legacy in our family. It started with just the two of us. Then, when our kids got older, it became the five of us. Now, our kids are grown with families of their own, so it's many more and counting.

So I ask you, starting right here, right now: What will you say? What will you choose to see? And how many lives might you change with your dream legacy?

YOUR DREAM PLAN

1. **Your Inspiration:** Seeing that former coach and teacher get an award for making $10,000 a month inspired me to dream more. If he could do it, I knew I could do it too.

   Think about your dream. Who are some people who have achieved similar dreams? Who inspires you? List their names here:

   You may want to take this further and reach out to these people if possible. Ask if you can interview them and discover how they did it. Use their stories to continue to fuel your dream.

2. **Say It:** It's time to say your dream out loud. Build your own Dream Script using the two simple parts. Write your best answer for your specific dream and your why below:

   - I choose to get in the game and pursue my dream of . . .

   - because . . .

You know what to do next: *Say it out loud!*

3. **See It:** Build your Dream Board! Grab a blank sheet of paper, piece of poster board, or even some cardboard, and start visualizing what your dream looks like. Use photographs, magazine clippings, printouts—whatever you have available as a medium—to craft a visual of what you're dreaming to achieve. If you really want to go all out, you can get a Dream Board kit online with pictures you can use. Whatever your dream is, capture it on your Dream Board, and set it up in a high-traffic spot in your home. Visualize it every time you walk by. It's your dream. Say it. See it. Achieve it!

Live on the Offense

*If you don't take risks for something different,
you guarantee more of the same.*

It was Day One for me. When the alarm clock went off on my last day of teaching, I jumped out of bed, energized by the thought that I would never have to wake up to an alarm again!

People at my school knew I was having success with my direct-selling business. A few of the teachers had even joined my team. But I don't think anyone expected me to leave teaching behind. Teaching was the safe bet, the guaranteed paycheck complete with health insurance. It was like playing good defense. I mean, who leaves a guaranteed job and the certainty that goes with it to step out into the unknown? That's not normal. Nevertheless, Cindy and I just knew we had to go on the offense and see how far we could go.

Earlier in the year, when we received our first $10,000 monthly check, the time had come to decide if I would stay in teaching or leave it behind. I'd just received a call from my friend Paul Orberson, who had sat with me in a Big Boy restaurant as I penciled out what we needed to make ends meet on the back of a place mat. "The ball is in your court, my friend," he challenged me. "You said you'd leave teaching once you hit this level. So what are you going to do now?"

I knew what I had to do. We had reached as high as we could go without focusing on the business full-time. It was now or never.

So one morning in the fall of 1995, I asked to meet with Principal MacFalone. While I waited in the lobby and silently rehearsed what I wanted to say, I felt a curious mix of nervousness and excitement. It felt more like preparing for my first day of school than arranging for my last day. When the time came for the meeting, I sat down in his office and said, "Brian—it's time for me to leave teaching."

The principal set down his pen and folded his hands together on his desk. "I kind of thought this was coming," he replied, a grin beginning to form on his otherwise serious face. "So, I take it you're doing well with your sales job?"

At that moment, I realized that I didn't really think of it as a job. "Yes, it's going well. And I'm at the point now that, if I don't go all in, I'll always wonder what could've happened."

He sighed and smiled. I had figured he would be supportive about the whole thing, and he was. "We're well into the first semester now," he pointed out. "I won't be able to get someone in to replace you until the second semester begins. Is there any chance we can keep you here through the end of the first semester?" I certainly didn't want to leave my peers or the kids in a tough spot, so I told him I'd be happy to stay until then.

When we were done discussing the details, Principal MacFalone stood up and shook my hand. "You've done some incredible work here, Coach. I hope you feel like it's all been worth it." Then he added, "And I hope you know what you're getting yourself into."

"Me too," I said as I turned to leave his office. As I shut the door behind me, I felt excited, like a weight had been lifted from me. I felt lighter than I had in decades. I felt the freedom to succeed or fail. Whatever it would be, it would all be up to Cindy and me.

———

As I backed out of the driveway on my last day of teaching school, the winter morning was still dark and cold. Yet even as my fingers gripped the frigid steering wheel on my final drive to work, I couldn't help but smile.

I parked in the spot I always tried to get near the gym. By this point, it was all starting to feel a little bittersweet. As I climbed out of the driver's seat, I paused for a moment to lean against the door and look at the gym where I had coached so many teams for so many years. In the previous season, the team had had an incredible run with eighteen wins and only two losses. Plus, all of my star players would be returning. That's not the kind of situation most coaches leave, but I knew the team was positioned to keep moving forward without me. As I grabbed the cold steel door handle and stepped inside the building, I admit I felt a few butterflies about leaving my job and following my dream. *Only eight more hours to go*, I thought.

I'd already cleaned out my classroom and coach's office, so my desk was pretty bare. I had to use a paper cup for my morning coffee because I'd already taken my favorite mug home. I set my briefcase down on the desk, hung my coat on the hook behind the door one last time, and walked toward the teachers' lounge. As students filled the hallway, the slamming of locker doors echoed around me. *This I might miss*, I thought. But I shut out that thought before entering the lounge.

The "breakfast club" was already there. (That's the nickname I'd given the teachers who liked to come in early and drink bad coffee while sitting in the lounge.) They were talking about all the usual stuff: the upcoming break, how many papers they had left to grade, the never-ending work of being a teacher. In that moment, it hit me—here I was stepping out on offense, and they were sitting there playing defense, just as they probably would be for many years to come.

"Last day, Coach?" someone asked.

I smiled and replied politely, "Yeah, it's here. Hard to believe." There was only enough coffee for half a cup, so I started making a new pot, just like I had done countless times before.

"I sure hope you aren't making a mistake," another teacher said as I waited for the coffee to brew.

"I don't think I am," I responded. "But I guess I won't know for sure until I get into it." *They are all good people,* I told myself. *They're just playing defense. I get it. I just don't want to do it anymore.* I grabbed the partially brewed pot and topped off my coffee cup. *It might be a little strong,* I thought, *but I'm ready to move on.*

"If I don't see you again before the end of the day," I said, holding my cup up and nodding my head at them as I left, "have a great rest of the year!"

As the door shut behind me, I heard one of them say, "He'll be back."

I shook my head and thought to myself, *I'll never be back.*

As I made my way to the classroom, I thought about how there was only one way to make more money in the school environment. If I continued there, I would have to move out of the classroom—the part I loved—and into an administrative role. That would get me a modest pay bump and some more vacation time. But, eventually, that would top out too. Then, after a thirty-five-year career, I supposed I could retire and that would be that.

Have you ever had a dream but chose what looked like a safer option that wouldn't be so hard to achieve? I know it might sound bad when I put it that way, but let's be honest—we all choose the path of least resistance at times because it's more comfortable. I could have stayed put, but what would I have had then? *A life well-lived—but on defense.* Safe, secure, and predictable. If that was my ultimate dream, then that would have been great. But deep down, I wanted more from life for myself and for my family.

At some point, maybe we would've moved to a nicer house in a nicer area of town, but I would've had a limited impact on my community. We wouldn't have been able to give our children educational opportunities to advance in life; we wouldn't have been able to move to our dream ranch in Florida; we wouldn't have been able to film a movie on that ranch; we wouldn't have been able to build churches, schools, and gymnasiums in struggling communities; we wouldn't have been able to sponsor families living through pediatric cancer treatments; and we wouldn't have been able to make significant donations to fund pediatric cancer research.

That last day of teaching flew by as I opened my math books, breathed in the smell of chalk dust in the air, and high-fived students as they left my classroom one last time. Some of them stopped by my desk to wish me luck and just chat a little. That choked me up. A few of my colleagues who were excited for me stopped by between classes, but for the most part, it was a pretty normal day—one of the last "normal" days I hoped I would ever experience.

When the last bell finally rang, I took one final look around my classroom before shutting off the lights and closing the door behind me. I heard the *click* of the door latch as I realized this would be the last time I would walk down these halls as a teacher. With my lunch box and briefcase in hand and a lot of memories in my heart, I strolled through the halls I'd walked down for the last sixteen years.

I paused by the gym door, listening to the sounds of shoes squeaking as players dashed back and forth on the court. I fought the urge to open those doors again, grab a whistle, and start coaching. Instead, I pushed through the metal doors to the parking lot, where a new beginning waited.

As I drove around the front of the school for the last time, my eyes lit up. There was my name on the school marquee! *How thoughtful,* I thought, and paused to read the farewell message: *Thank you Mark Pentecost for 16 years of teachening.* Since I was a math teacher, I had to read it twice to make sure my eyes weren't playing tricks on me. Nope, they had actually misspelled the word *teaching!*

I got quite a laugh out of that—it put the cherry on top of my entire teaching career. Quite literally, this was as good a sign as any that it was time to take the risk and start living on the offense, even though what came next would be all new. Because if you don't risk for something that's different, you guarantee yourself more of the same.

THE UNCERTAINTY OF CERTAINTY

The Dream Phenomenon is designed to gain momentum as you move through it. I hope you're as excited as I am about what's next for you—step 3: Live on the Offense.

Now, some people may hear my story and think, *Well, it worked out for you, Mark, but it might not work out like that for me.* And that's true. It might not work out *the same way.* But the key is that I was willing to take the risk for something different and not fall in love with more of the same—even though it looked a lot like certainty.

We need to think differently about *certainty.* Certainty is part of a *defensive* mindset. Many people think there is certainty in having a job, but that simply is not true. The truth is, the economy could shift at any time. Industries change every day. Companies go out of business or downsize. The reality is that there is always risk, no matter what path you choose. Staying put is risky. Stepping out is risky. It's not a question of whether you will have risk but *what* risk you will choose to embrace.

Like I said in the first chapter, people are often scared of doing the wrong thing when what they should be scared of is doing nothing. Doing nothing while feeling secure can be riskier than doing something that feels uncertain in the moment. For me, I knew I had to shift from living life on defense to living on offense when I realized that doing nothing at all was my riskiest move.

People often get stuck on the idea of not taking risks to better themselves because they don't want to lose job benefits such as health insurance coverage or paid vacation days. They also mistakenly think those are secure or guaranteed benefits. But what happens when an employer has to cut costs and starts slashing those benefits? They're not *actually* guaranteed. Sure, they might be nice to have, but that's why they're called *benefits*, not *certainties*.

So what will you miss out on in life if you stay on the defense? Maybe the real question is this: *If you slapped a* For Sale *sign on your dream and parked it at the curb, what would you be willing to sell it for?*

BAD RISK OR GOOD RISK?

Maybe we need to think differently about risk. Many of us associate risk with something bad. That perception keeps us living in a defensive mindset. Maybe we tried to do something different in the past and it didn't work out, or there were negative consequences. Because of one or two painful experiences, we've decided all risks are bad. That's simply not true.

There is Bad Risk, for sure. Bad Risk includes doing the same thing you've always done yet expecting a different result. (That's also the definition of insanity—and yes, Bad Risk *is* insane!) By taking that approach, you guarantee losing more of one thing we humans can never get back: *time.* In five years, in one year, or even in one month, you'll end up more frustrated and still stuck in the same place you are now.

But there is also Good Risk. When Cindy and I risked one night a week to make more cash, we decided how much time we were willing to invest in something new. If it hadn't worked out, we would've lost only that one night each week. In other words, we kept our potential losses to a minimum. I didn't quit my job. We didn't sell everything we had and sleep on the streets while hoping to make extra money. Obviously, that would have been a Bad Risk. We had to choose what we were willing to give up to go up.

Likewise, you have to determine what you are willing and able to lose. A little comfort? One night a week? The time you invest to start your blog or take an online course that can move your career to the next level?

Another example of Bad Risk is simply saying, "I'm going to quit my job today and try something new" without researching the new path and making an informed decision. Good Risk is taking action—but only once you've done your homework. It's not haphazardly leaping before you look. If you spend your free time researching what you need to do to take that next step and *then* plan, you reduce the Bad Risk and increase the Good Risk.

Cindy and I knew the exact amount of money we needed before I could walk away from teaching because we had done our homework. Your number will be different and unique to your own situation. To figure out our family's number, we created a budget. We researched the cost of health insurance and the other benefits we received from my teaching job. We carefully built and supported our sales team. It took about two years for me to go from "Maybe someday I can leave teaching" to "I *am* leaving teaching."

That doesn't mean your decisions are cold, calculated, and emotionless. Good Risk is not the absence of emotion and passion. Instead, it's the power of passion and emotion focused intentionally by research and planning. It's taking control of your life and living on offense—grabbing the ball and driving down the court.

Some people think they can avoid taking risks and doing all that planning by simply hoping to get lucky. First, I don't believe in luck. I believe in hard work and follow-through. You can create your own opportunities if you don't wait around for luck to do the work for you.

What about the people who buy the winning lottery ticket, and it changes their lives? Didn't they get lucky? I'm glad you brought that up because I always say that buying a lottery ticket is a cheap way to keep your dreams alive. If you're not an Active Dreamer, it's a chance to flex your Dream Muscle, if only for five minutes, while you think about what you'd do with your winnings. But it's a Bad Risk because, instead of actually acting on your dreams, you're just daydreaming. The odds of winning a Powerball lottery are about one in almost three hundred million.[12] That's almost the entire population of the United States! You'll be waiting a long time for your dreams to come true if they depend on you picking a winning number.

Even if you did win the lottery, it wouldn't change the amount of planning or work you'd still have to put in to achieve your dreams. Suppose a lottery winner has a dream to open a dog rescue center. Winning the lottery doesn't mean that person wakes up the next morning and magically owns a dog rescue center. They still have to research the business, find the right people for their team, secure the property, build facilities, and much more if they want that dream to become reality. In and of itself, getting money doesn't make things happen.

Unfortunately, the sad news is that a lot of people who do win the lottery soon go bankrupt. That reveals something important: When people are simply handed what they think their dreams are without having to take the risk to achieve them, they often fail to appreciate them. Plus, they don't grow along the way to become the kind of person who is prepared to handle success, because they're still living on defense. As a result, they revert to old habits and take Bad Risks, which can lead directly to bankruptcy.

I realize no two stories are the same, but the Good Risk required to achieve your dreams only happens when you do the work and live on the offense.

THE RISK TABLE

There's no such thing as a risk-free life. Whatever decision you make, whether it's to do nothing or to chase your dream, is a risk. Even your dreams can and do change. They evolve with you as you grow. The beauty is that you get to choose your risk.

Bad Risk is when we either do nothing or don't do what we should do to prepare for success. We don't plan, research, or otherwise get ready to make an informed decision and act. We might jump in simply because we had an emotional response, like getting frustrated one too many times at our job and quitting on the spot without a plan for what happens next. If a basketball player launched a shot from half-court with three minutes still left in the game, that would be a Bad Risk, because there was still plenty of time to get better chances to score.

On the other hand, Good Risk takes time. Good Risk is patient and planned, but it still requires action.

It challenges you to take control of the ball and drive down the court for your shot to win the game. Or if there are only three seconds left in the game instead of three minutes, shooting the ball from half-court might be a calculated Good Risk! Standing there doing nothing would not be a wise move.

If you get stuck in the planning and researching stage and are afraid to act, you've drifted from Good Risk to Bad Risk, from offense to defense. But that's where your passion for your dream can fuel your next step.

Good and Bad Risk are often opposites, as you can see from the following Risk Table:

Good Risk	Bad Risk
Recoverable	Catastrophic
Calculated	Luck
Logical	Impulsive
Transparent	Hidden
Clarity	Ambiguity

Let's take a closer look at these pairings.

- **Recoverable vs. Catastrophic:** You can bounce back and recover from taking Good Risk, but Bad Risk can leave you in a hole so huge you struggle to find any opportunity to dream again. Often, you can make more progress in the long term by taking recoverable risks that are sure to move you forward, even if you fall short of your goal.
- **Calculated vs. Luck:** Buying a lottery ticket and hoping is not a great strategy for seeing your dreams come to life. My decision to leave teaching wasn't based on hoping I'd get lucky and make more money. I had a calculated plan in place to keep achieving success. Don't just roll the dice; make a plan.
- **Logical vs. Impulsive:** Believe me, there is a place for passion and emotion to fuel and sustain you on this dream journey, but begin with thinking rationally about what your steps will be. Clearheaded thinking goes a long way in guiding energetic excitement.
- **Transparent vs. Hidden:** Good Risk is straightforward and authentic, both with yourself and with others. Bad Risk causes you to feel like you have to hide things because

something inside you just knows something is off. Maybe you don't want to hear what others have to say about it because you suspect they might be right. I'm not saying you have to tell everyone all of your dreams, but beware when you don't feel free to share them with people you trust.

- **Clarity vs. Ambiguity:** There's nothing like fuzziness to make your dream difficult to bring to life. If you are not clear on your path, you'll struggle to know which step to take next. Clarity accelerates your chances of success because a clear dream is an achievable dream.

What happens if I do all of that planning and work to increase my Good Risk—and I still fail? That seems like a Bad Risk in disguise. To that I say, look at Michael Jordan.

When you think about risk, you probably don't think about Michael Jordan. After all, he is one of the greatest basketball players of all time, so you might think success came easily to him. But do you have any idea how many shots he *missed* over the course of his basketball career? Nine thousand! That's right—a professional athlete credited for the championship dream run of the Chicago Bulls *missed* more than nine thousand shots.[13]

That sounds like what most people think of as a Bad Risk, doesn't it? Apparently not. In fact, trying and *failing* nine thousand times became his path to greatness. Imagine if he had quit basketball after missing his first shot as a professional athlete. We only know about him because he didn't give up after one failure.

So if you put in the work, and it doesn't work out perfectly the first time, that does not mean it was a Bad Risk. Think about Michael Jordan, reevaluate things, and try it again. The only time you really fail is if you stop chasing your dream.

OUTSIDE YOUR COMFORT ZONE

Good Risk often requires stepping into what makes you uncomfortable. Not too long after leaving teaching, Cindy and I made that move from Allegan to Grand Rapids. To give you an idea of the jump we made, the population of Grand Rapids was about fifty times that of Allegan. We went from being pretty well-known fish in a little pond to average fish in a big pond. Instead of our neighbors being other teachers and blue-collar workers, they were multi-million-dollar-earning investment bankers and business owners.

Because everything was changing so fast, we often didn't think about the risks we were taking at this point. But moving towns and houses, expanding our team, and starting to mingle with new social groups also forced us out of our comfort zones. We were now working with people who had more money and influence.

When we first branched out into Chicago, I headed into the city once a week to develop a sales team. One of the first times I was down there to host an in-home meeting, I thought I might've gotten the address wrong. I pulled up to a gated community, where I gave an attendant the address. He announced my arrival before he gave me directions to the house and opened the gates to the neighborhood. As I drove slowly through the winding streets, I strained my neck as I stared at the houses, my mouth hanging open. These were

HUDDLE UP!

When you're on the offense, you've got to shoot your shot. So get yourself a scoreboard, and start making those shots. You can simply keep track on your phone, on a portable dry-erase whiteboard, or even with a real electronic scoreboard you buy online. Whenever you go on offense, take a step forward, or achieve a milestone toward your dream, give yourself a point—or a hundred points! It's up to you. Just make sure you use this scoreboard as a constant visual reminder of the need to stay on offense.

massive, multimillion-dollar properties. To an outsider like me, these were people who had "made it."

When I finally found the house—or mansion, really—I parked my car, grabbed my briefcase, and walked up the steps to knock on the large front door. A butler answered. *A butler!* Our new neighborhood in Grand Rapids was nice, but I didn't know anyone who had a butler.

The husband was an influential attorney in Chicago, and the wife wanted to join my team. She wanted to show that she could make money too. We hit it off right away, and I started meeting more of their friends and going to different social events. Let's just say I felt out of my league for a while. One evening, they took me to a happy hour in Highland Park. There, I met celebrities such as the great Chicago Bulls basketball players Michael Jordan and Scottie Pippen. It was an incredible experience! I thought the best part was that they served some of the biggest shrimp I'd ever seen. I love a good shrimp cocktail, and I must have gotten carried away because—horror of horrors—at some point, I double-dipped my shrimp into the cocktail sauce. For Christmas that year, that couple graciously gave me a gift I apparently desperately needed: an etiquette book! We enjoyed a good laugh about that for years to come.

The strangest part of all of this was that here I was, a former basketball coach and math teacher, meeting with successful people. Yet I was the one giving *them* the confidence to start their own businesses.

Every time Cindy and I put ourselves out there, we built our Dream Muscle a little more. It would've been easy to stop, because the constant push for growth could be overwhelming at times. But we knew by then that if the bubble ever burst, we'd be able to recreate our success. We had already done it once. If we were willing to take the risk and get uncomfortable, we could do it again.

THE ENEMY

Having seen how the fear of risk held us back in our early years and how it held back so many people I've met and coached since then, here is what I would tell my younger self: *Make risk your friend by realizing certainty is your enemy.*

In fact, I'd go so far as to say that wanting what looks like certainty has doomed more dreams than anything else. Because you simply can't get to where you want to go without Good Risk. You must live on the offense.

When I started my basketball coaching career, I was big on playing defense. If you follow sports, you hear this expression a lot: "Defense wins championships." Sometimes, that's true. In the town of Allegan, we always had a small pool of basketball players. And at any given time, only a few of the eleven players on the team were great athletes. We had to rely on the one or two great ones and figure out how to minimize the deficiencies of the other players. But that kind of thinking didn't lead me to coach *to win*, just *not to lose*. I soon realized we had to get creative to find ways to win.

That's when I decided to try something different. One night, instead of focusing on our regular defense, we kept pressing the other team and aggressively going on the offense when we had the ball. Every time we got control of the ball, we pushed it up the court, passing and dribbling, driving to the basket again and again.

When we made that adjustment, everything changed. The energy in the gym skyrocketed. The crowd got excited. The athletes got excited. *I got excited.* We began to gain momentum both in that game and for the rest of the season. Instead of simply trying not to lose, we shifted our focus. We played to win. The powerful switch from defense to offense enabled us to create a greater margin of error. We won more games than ever—and never looked back.

When you're doing all you can to live in perceived certainty, you're living on the defensive. If you live on the defensive, you choose to live that "normal" life, just trying not to lose. You live life on your heels, constantly reacting to what life gives you.

Live on the offense, and you control your own destiny. As a dreamer, this lifestyle soon becomes your new normal. You live life with energy on the balls of your feet, moving forward instead of waiting to see what life sends your way. You choose to be proactive, not reactive. As you seize your opportunities, you drive them down the court of life, finding ways to overcome any obstacles in your way.

When I made the shift from living on the defense to living on the offense and taking Good Risks, I had no idea how good things could get. When we realized we could make risk our friend, Cindy and I began to create our own opportunities and developed incredible momentum. It was as if we could hear the fans in the stands cheering us on as we played hard, took risks, and celebrated our wins.

MAKING DREAM RIPPLES

The best part of living on the offense, though, isn't about you or me; it's about the ripple effect our dreams can have on others when we're willing to take Good Risks.

I saw this happen when I had a dream to film a Western feature-length film, *Florida Wild*, on our ranch in Florida. Most studios would not film a movie in Florida because there are no incentives to film there like there are in other states, but we thought it was a Good Risk, even though it did not make sense financially. It was, after all, a Florida story, and I wanted it to be as authentic as possible. Plus, it would be a lot of fun!

What we discovered was that it meant a lot to other people too. At one of the wrap parties after we finished filming, the cast and crew gave me an old lunch box containing handwritten messages. The next day, I read the heartfelt notes, which explained what being part of the making of the movie had meant to them.

One crew member was a retired carpenter from the area who had always wanted to work on a movie set but had never been able to travel to another state to do it. Not only was he able to work on the set, but he got to do it with his grandson. Others said they were able to pay off their debt and more with the earnings from the production. A few more people said they'd always had the dream of being an extra on a film as a cowboy or riding a horse in a Western film, and this production let them do that. So many people wrote that it had been a once-in-a-lifetime experience for them. And they were only able to achieve those dreams because we took the risk and filmed in Florida.

Here I was thinking that this film was *my* dream when, in reality, it was also a dream fulfilled for the people who worked on the film.

Living on the offense is what creates that powerful ripple effect. Being willing to leave certainty behind and chase your dream impacts the lives of those around you and those who help you. And that's what I want for you. I want you to be able to celebrate because you took the risk, achieved the win, and brought others with you. Think about it: When was the last time you saw someone play it safe—and then throw a party to celebrate it?

In football, playing it safe might mean running what is called a "prevent defense." The aim is to give the other team room to make limited gains but keep them from scoring enough points to win before time runs out. Unfortunately, that strategy often backfires. Plus, I have never seen the team playing defense do an end-zone dance. That only happens when someone scores a touchdown and does some crazy celebration in the end zone. Other players get involved. Fans love it. It brings the energy to *a whole 'notha level*! But only the team that plays on offense gets to do those end-zone dances.

I encourage you to make Good Risk your friend. Do your homework, then go ahead and step out. Not only will you generate dream ripples in the world around you, but you will also create more opportunities to celebrate success.

YOUR DREAM PLAN

1. **Confront your fears.** It can be easy to let your fears or worries control your actions. Think about a situation that has you worried. As you evaluate what seems risky about it, ask yourself these three questions:

   - What's keeping you on the defensive? Go ahead and write those fears here:

   - If you choose to do nothing, what might happen?

   - What might happen if you go on the offense?

2. **Convert Bad Risk to Good Risk.** Revisit the Risk Table and consider how you might convert your fears of Bad Risk into Good Risk possibilities.

   For example, suppose one of your fears is that if you stepped away from your current job, you lose your health insurance and then get sick. You might see that as a catastrophic Bad Risk. So how could you make it a recoverable Good Risk? What if you found a way to make enough money to buy your own health insurance—perhaps with a higher deductible—that cost you less? That might minimize the risk of making your next best move.

Now, it's your turn. Whatever your fears may be, use the following Risk Table options to come up with ways to convert your Bad Risk to Good Risk.

Good Risk	Bad Risk
Recoverable	Catastrophic
Calculated	Luck
Logical	Impulsive
Transparent	Hidden
Clarity	Ambiguity

My fear of Bad Risk is:

Here's how I might convert that Bad Risk into Good Risk:

Get Back Up

*There's no such thing as work that is
hard, only work that is worth it.*

Cindy and I built a business, made all the money
we wanted, and lived happily ever after in
Florida as multimillionaires. There you go. That's
the Dream Phenomenon! The end.

Boy, if that were the rest of the story, this would
be a much shorter book. But that's not how it happened because that's not how the Dream Phenomenon works. The truth is that the path to achieving
your dream isn't a straight line that always goes up.
Whether your dream is to wake up without an alarm
clock or to make a million dollars, I guarantee you'll
have a lot of ups and downs.

When some people see me now, they say, "Mark, you're so lucky this has all worked out." I have to laugh. If they only knew how many times I've had to get back up, they would know it had very little to do with luck and everything to do with resilience.

If you're on this journey with me, the same thing will happen to you. When we meet, no matter what anyone else thinks, you and I will know what went on behind the scenes. Maybe we dreamers should give each other a silent nod or have a secret handshake as a sign to show we know what really went into making our dreams come true.

This step—Get Back Up—is one of the most important moves to master. Trust me, you'll need this one again and again. No one gets to the top without challenges. With this step, I'm giving you the armor you'll need to stand strong when things don't go the way you hoped they would. Don't get me wrong—your dream journey will be fun, but it will not always be easy.

If you haven't experienced any setbacks yet as you pursue your dream, you will. You can count on it. But what if every time you thought you hit a ceiling, you just *knew* without a doubt that you'd bust through it? Imagine what would be possible for you if you learned to turn your setbacks into setups for comebacks.

Two years after I left teaching, potential setbacks arrived. The industry our business was in began to change dramatically. Different long-distance carriers began offering even lower rates, which made it impossible to make money. As technology changed, the company tried selling pagers (Haha! Do you even know what a pager is?), but people didn't need them once they started using cell phones. It all ended abruptly when I was asked to promote the company to new customers and business partners as if everything were looking great for future growth. When I declined, the company broke all ties with us.

Just like that, we were out on our own without the income we had worked so hard to build.

That was the first big punch to the gut. Our phenomenal run in that first business lasted six years. I had left teaching to grow the business, then *boom!*— it was gone.

We had a choice: We could resign ourselves to the setback and go back to teaching, or we could let the setback set us up for a comeback. We chose the comeback.

Cindy and I had learned enough about business and earned enough money to invest in our next big dream: starting our own business. We wanted to better control our own destiny. We had explored a few different product options when an old acquaintance asked us to become marketers for a new product with a new company. What the product promised to do sounded ridiculous to us at the time, so she sent us a sample to try. When we opened the box we received from her, all the instructions were in Spanish, and we could only read English. We eventually figured out it was a body wrap designed to help people improve their health and wellness by toning and tightening their physique. At that time, you could only get a body wrap like that in a luxury spa.

Cindy and I tried them out for a few days, and we were *shocked* at how effective they were! "It works!" I shouted to Cindy.

The product was great, but the company hadn't yet established the business savvy or sales and marketing to support it. We saw an opportunity, but we didn't want a repeat of our previous punch-in-the-gut experience. We wanted to be owners, so we partnered with the man who made the wraps to begin a new company with the only name that seemed to fit: It Works!

When we started It Works!, we were determined to give it everything, no matter what setbacks came our way. We were excited and terrified and ecstatic and anxious—all at the same time.

WORK THAT'S WORTH IT

We faced a lot of potential setbacks along the way, but one that stands out to me came around Christmas of 2007. Doug, our original and longtime chief financial officer at It Works!, asked me to stop by his office one evening. I had known Doug and his wife from my days working in education. Even though I'd left teaching, Doug continued to teach during the day, then drove about forty-five minutes to Grand Rapids in the evenings to work with me. Over the years, he and I had become close friends.

That evening in his office, however, Doug didn't look ready to party. He took off his glasses, rubbed the bridge of his nose, and then paused before saying, "Mark, this isn't working." I must have looked confused, so he clarified. "It Works! It just isn't working."

As I stared at him across the sea of papers on his desk, I just blinked, still not grasping what he was saying. "How much do you need for payroll?" I asked. I was ready to sign a check from my personal account to cover the expenses.

"No, Mark, you don't understand." Doug sighed wearily. "It's not working." I leaned back in my chair and gave him a puzzled look. "Mark, I'm taking off my CFO hat right now," he said, "and I'm putting on my friendship hat."

I nodded to let him know I was tracking with him.

"When are you going to say *enough*?" Doug leaned forward across the stacks of papers. "You're losing all the money you made in direct sales. You've got lines of credit on all your buildings. When are you going to call it quits?"

In many ways, I thought I had become numb to setbacks, but this one felt different. I realized this conversation could not have been easy for Doug. He knew we'd worked so hard to get here.

As always, I just answered honestly. "I haven't thought of it," I told him. It was true. The thought of quitting had never entered my mind.

"I just don't want to see you bury yourself."

There was an awkward pause while I processed what he was saying.

"I appreciate you," I finally said. "I know it must've been tough for you to have this conversation with me. But we're so close, Doug. It Works! is so close to hitting it big."

He leaned back in his chair and pointed to the papers in front of him. "But Mark, look at the numbers. We're losing more than we're making, and you keep having to put more and more money in to keep the business afloat. When will you quit?"

At that moment, I had a choice. I could agree with Doug's assessment and say, "You're right, Doug. We're done here." Or I could get back up and find a way to make a comeback. I knew we had people counting on the company. It wasn't just my family; it was the family of every salesperson, warehouse worker, and leader associated with us.

"Let's give it a few more months and see what we can do," I told Doug. As we finished our conversation, I don't think we had the clarity he might have wanted, but I also didn't think our company's time was up.

One thing was obvious to me: The clock was running out. I knew hard work was exactly what it would take, but I also knew this: There's no such thing as work that is hard, only work that is worth it. When you believe your work is worth it to achieve your *why*, everything gets easier to do. And I thought It Works! was worth it.

The Resiliency-Relationship Connection

Did you know your relationships can position you to be more resilient in the face of adversity? According to a *Harvard Business Review* study, the strength of your relationships and network can help set you up for resilience *before* the going gets tough.[14] Researchers identified eight areas in which well-developed relationships can make us more resilient:

1. **Work:** Relationships help us shift and manage when professional challenges surge.
2. **Pushback:** Relationships help us find the confidence to self-advocate in the face of adversity.
3. **Vision:** Relationships help us see the path forward.
4. **Perspective:** Relationships help us see the big picture when setbacks come.
5. **Purpose:** Relationships remind us of the reason and meaning in what we do.
6. **Humor:** Relationships help us laugh at ourselves and our situations.
7. **People:** Relationships help us make sense of the personal dynamics in a situation.
8. **Empathy:** Relationships support us so we can release or process emotions.

I realized that I could either quit or pivot. So we changed our strategy. We equipped some of the sales reps to meet and greet people at various conventions, expos, and conferences. We added new team members in Arizona who saw the vision and started going after it from day one. I traveled around to our teams to let them know we were there to support them.

Then we got creative and unveiled a little friendly internal competition. The highest-selling leader would achieve a new Ambassador tier in our company and win an all-inclusive trip to a tropical destination. Plus, they'd get their picture in our first ever It Works! Hall of Fame. I personally reached out to the people who I thought could win and challenged them to go for it. I helped them create goals and visualize their success. And you know what happened? We had many people energized and striving to reach that Ambassador level!

All these moves helped push us past the resistance and created the momentum we needed to break through. Even when it seemed our time was up and it didn't make sense to keep going, I chose to get back up. But if Doug hadn't sat me down that day and delivered that friendly punch in the gut, who knows how long it would've taken us to make It Works! the success it became? I didn't want to hear it, but it pushed us into success faster.

Thanks to the work we put in after my conversation with Doug, the business was finally taking off—until we ran into a problem we could not fix quickly: The suppliers of our signature wraps couldn't keep up with demand. We couldn't make the wraps fast enough. We had no problem selling them. We had problems delivering what we sold.

I don't know if you've noticed, but when times are tough, most people's first reaction is to quit. When the going gets tough, a lot of people choose what *looks* like an easier route, but it's really an escape hatch. The same is true for you. When you face adversity, your first instinct might be to drop out or choose a path that looks easier.

So many team members worked their tails off during that challenging time. The ones who stayed with us built their resilience. They discovered they were able to meet any setback and rise above it.

HUDDLE UP!

Imagine you are going in what you believe to be the right direction when someone you trust tells you, "It's not working." What would you do? Quit? Shrug it off? Cry? (You don't have to admit that last one.) The solution may be to strategize, pivot, or get creative. One thing is certain: If you want to overcome the challenge, you'll need to tap into your resilience to elevate your focus and keep moving forward! Remember, you have to be *in* the game to *win* the game.

In fact, some of them got so good because of it that they soon joined The Millionaires' Club at our company.

Whenever we face a potential setback, I like to name and embrace the challenge so I can choose what to say about it and how to see it. Flipping the narrative on a potential setback is the key to turning it into a setup for a comeback.

So we called this "The Great Wrap Shortage of 2008." We flipped the narrative to see the shortage not as a problem but as a testament to how popular our product was. We never stopped taking orders. Instead, we invited people to sign up to wait in line for the next available wraps—like waiting in line for the next iPhone release. *They're so good, we can't keep 'em in stock!*

Another major challenge came a couple of years later when we decided to upgrade our entire information and accounting system. We hired a great IT company and invested two years into the process of making the move. But right before the switch, the IT company was bought out by private equity. Everything simply was not in place to ensure a smooth transfer.

As a result, our entire IT system went down. I mean, it totally failed. We couldn't add customers. We couldn't add sales reps. We couldn't place orders. People got charged double or even triple what they had agreed to buy. Everything that could have gone wrong *did* go wrong. The only way we could do any business was to go old school and have people call the main office to speak directly with someone by phone to manually enter their information.

At first, we thought it might take twenty-four hours to resolve. Then days became weeks, and weeks became months. Once again, however, we chose to see it as a setup for a comeback. We framed the setback as an opportunity to serve together and earn It Works! Medals of Honor.

When our IT issues were finally fixed, we felt invincible. Learning how to be resilient together made us stronger and positioned us for the growth that was yet to come. In fact, the people who stayed with us through the tough times ended up staying with the company for many years. Some of them are still with us today.

Over the years, I've found something to be true. I say it so much that my friends call it the Pent Way for my nickname of "Pent": The amount of work you're willing to put into something directly correlates to what you get out of it. Put more work in, and you'll get more good stuff out. It's simple and, even better, it's guaranteed.

I can't tell you what your struggles might be. I just know they *will* come. When they do, remember that they are only *potential* setbacks. They only truly become setbacks if you let them.

After taking this journey with me so far, I hope you've started dreaming again. I hope you've made a Dream Board and that you're ready to go on the offense. But what will happen when your own potential setbacks come? What will you do when:

- Your business partner suddenly quits on you?
- Your health takes a hit or your kids get sick?
- You run out of cash to keep the bills paid and the lights on?
- You _____?
  (Just fill in the blank with whatever it is here.)

When life punches you in the gut, will you quit? Or will you remember your *why* and get back up, knowing all the work will be worth it? When that little voice in your head tells you it's impossible, will you listen to it and shut down your dreams? Or will you flip the narrative and tell yourself a different story of resilience?

I can tell you right now that getting back up is worth it—because all it takes to succeed in the face of challenges is a little math.

THE RESILIENCE QUOTIENT

As a former math teacher, I came up with a simple formula—the Resilience Quotient (RQ)—to express the power of getting back up. Here's how it works: Simply divide the number of times you *are willing to get back up* by the number of times you *will get knocked down.*

Resilience Quotient =

$$\frac{\text{\# of times you're \underline{willing} to get up}}{\text{\# of times you \underline{will} get knocked down}}$$

If your RQ is greater than 1, you're good. If your RQ is less than 1, you're done. That's pretty simple. The lack of a positive RQ is what keeps many people from ever realizing their dreams. When they get knocked down, they stay down. Their RQ is < 1. But you're different.

It's never a question of *will* you get knocked down; it's a matter of *when*. You simply must be willing to get back up *one more time*. I know it doesn't sound flashy, but it is the truth. In fact, I'd go so far as to say that my RQ is what kept me in the game long enough to give me a chance to win.

You expect to get knocked down because that is proof that you are in the game. I've never seen a player sitting on the bench get knocked down by the other team. Only the ones in the game get that privilege.

Got knocked down today? Get back up today. RQ > 1.

And the next time, do the same thing.

Every. Single. Time.

As long as you're willing to get back up, your dream *cannot* die. And every time you get back up, something amazing happens: Your Dream Muscle gets stronger. Every time it gets stronger, it gets easier to believe getting back up is worth it.

Now, it does take time and repetition to build that resilience. That's why I emphasize the need to have a strong *why* to help fuel your drive to get back up again. So give yourself some grace and say, "Today, my RQ is greater than 1." And then get up one more time.

This reminds me of one of my favorite movies, *Rocky*, starring Sylvester Stallone. When we first meet Rocky, he's fighting just enough to get paid, and that's about it. He's lost his hunger for life and isn't interested in being anything more

HUDDLE UP!

If you haven't already done this, I want to challenge you to add something to your Dream Board: your *why*. If Cindy and I hadn't been laser-focused on our *why*, we would have struggled to face the challenges in the early years of It Works! Right now, you may be the only person invested in your dream, even if it will eventually benefit more people than just you. You need to believe in what you're doing with all your heart and keep your *why* front and center to help you rise above the setbacks.

than he already is. But then Apollo Creed's manager calls and wants him for the big fight. Not only will Rocky get the biggest payday of his life, but he'll also get something he's never had before: a shot at the title.

We see Rocky training—first by himself and then with Mickey as his trainer. We see the famous montage that ends with Rocky running up the steps of the Philadelphia Museum of Art, punching the air at the top because he knows he can go the distance. When he and Creed fight, they go for all fifteen excruciating rounds. They each go down at different points in the bout, but Rocky refuses to quit. He stays in the ring until the final bell. In doing so, he shows us that winning wasn't really all about the title but about choosing to get back up each and every time.

As I reflected on that key conversation I had with Doug, I realized he was my Mickey—a person in my corner I could trust to look out for me and the company. But I also knew I could not just tap out. I needed to keep going. I needed to go the distance. By staying focused despite adversity, we doubled down and reinvented ourselves to become a more successful company than Doug and I ever could have predicted back then.

I've had a lot of Mickeys in my corner over the years. In my own family, I've had my wife, Cindy, and my three children, Kami, Kindsey, and Kyler—all of whom have encouraged me to dream and have inspired me to reach for more on those days when the going got tough.

In business, I've had people in my corner such as Larry, who wrote a check to help get It Works! started, and Luis, who partnered with us to create our core product with nothing more than a handshake deal. As my business grew, I knew that my knowledge needed to grow with it. I relied on people like Keith to bring expertise to my corner for everything I didn't know but needed to. I couldn't have done any of it without all of my team who made the commitment and relocated to Florida with me. Then there were the friends and spiritual advisors who have helped me navigate setbacks—people like Jerry, Stuart, Chris, and Jentezen.

The list goes on. Each of these people—and many more—have been in my corner when the going got tough. So who is in your corner? Who are your Mickeys, the people who will tell you the truth and help you get back up when challenges knock you down? Look for those people who will encourage you when potential setbacks come.

When you have others to support you, you realize you don't need to be a superhuman to bring the Dream Phenomenon to life. You just need an RQ > 1. Always choose to get back up *one more time*.

YOUR DREAM PLAN

1. **Respond to adversity.** How do you typically respond to adversity? Maybe this is the first time you've thought about it, so ask yourself these questions:

   - Have you ever quit anything when the going got tough? Knowing what you know now, what would you have done differently?

   - Think about the Pent Way: *The amount of work you're willing to put into something directly correlates to what you get out of it.* Were you willing to put in the work when the going got tough, or was the work just not worth it to you?

   - Now use your imagination to look forward. In what ways might your *why* inspire you to push through the resistance in the future to turn your setbacks into setups for a comeback?

2. **Trust the right people.** Doug was my Mickey during my own dream journey; I trusted he was looking out for me and the company.

  - Who can be some of your Mickeys as you pursue your dream? Who will always be in your corner, encouraging you to keep getting back up after you've been punched in the gut? Who can come to you with an honest conversation and have your best interests at heart?

  - On the other hand, who is your Rocky? Who inspires you to keep getting back up with the example of resilience they've set for you?

3. **Frame your setbacks.** You can choose how you frame any *potential* setback that comes your way. You can choose to wallow in self-pity, or you can see it as an opportunity to make a comeback. You can fall into a negative perspective, or you can choose to emphasize the positive potential in every situation.

Think about a setback you are facing now or one that has come your way recently.

- What creative name can you give it (like "The Great Wrap Shortage")?

- How can you flip the narrative in a way that positions you and those around you to choose a more positive attitude about it?

Find Your People

*When planted in the RIGHT
environment, dreams THRIVE.*

*When planted in the WRONG
environment, dreams DIE.*

As you know by now, I love basketball. For those who don't know the game, a team can only have five players on the court at any time. The players a coach wants on the floor to start the game are the five who best position a team for success. That's why they're called the starting five.

Your Starting Five are the people you spend the most time with, the ones who complete you. That's why I call them *influencers*—not because they make cool videos for social media but because these are the people you choose to have the most influence on you as you grow on your dream journey.

Your Starting Five create an environment that either supports or derails your dreams because the people you surround yourself with will directly determine your success. These people shape what you talk about, what projects you work on, and what dreams you choose to pursue. That's why you need to Find Your People. When planted in the right environment, dreams thrive; when planted in the wrong environment, dreams die.

The members of my Starting Five have changed over the years, but I always seek people who excel at whatever I'm interested in so I can soak up their wisdom. When I was starting out in real estate, I needed someone who knew real estate. When I was starting a new company, I needed someone who knew start-ups. Now, I need someone who believes in my dreams and will help me accomplish them. I need someone who will bring energy and encourage me to keep getting back up. I need someone to listen without judgment and offer moral guidance in life.

Steve has been with me from the beginning of It Works!, even doing janitorial work until we could find a role for him. He's worn almost every hat in the company and excels at simply figuring out whatever needs to be figured out. Charlie brings infectious energy and optimism. He always sees the glass as half full, not half empty, and pushes me to keep giving all I have to bring my dreams to life.

I don't want all cheerleaders, however, and neither should you. You need people who are willing to tell you no. That's where Jerry comes in. For many years, I've known I can bring him problems, and he'll come back with perspectives I need to see but would never have thought of myself. He's not afraid to poke holes in my plans to help me avoid painful missteps.

Chris is a confidant, someone I can talk to about anything and know it will go no further. If I'm frustrated with people or situations, I know I have a safe place to share what I'm feeling and not feel judged. I turned to Keith repeatedly back when It Works! was first growing because of his track record of building large companies. He has shown me the tactical details of how to make things happen many times over the years.

They all make me a better person. They empower me to lean in to what I do best. I could simply read books about every challenge and find a way to do everything myself, but constantly trying to find solutions on my own would wear me out. My Starting Five improve my mental health, lower my stress level, and raise my belief level. They set me up to be fully present for the people I care about most.

To show how important my Starting Five are to me, I schedule time on my calendar for them. After all, if I'm not actually surrounding myself with them, they can't influence me to grow and change in a healthy way. By making time for them, I create an environment in which my dreams thrive.

The people in your own Starting Five will change over time, depending on what you need most in that season. Back when I coached basketball, I formed my Starting Five based on what I needed then. The local police chief was my assistant coach who brought energy and toughness. Another friend was my go-to for finding a way to get things done. I enlisted the help of a retired coach in his eighties to teach me all I didn't know. And the list goes on. It's amazing how quickly the Starting Five can come together in any season of life when

> **HUDDLE UP!**
>
> Harvard researcher and psychologist Dr. David McClelland studied people over several decades and found that as much as 95 percent of our success and failure is determined by the people we spend the most time with. One reason this happens is because of *neural synchronization*. As we spend time with someone, the neurons in different regions of our brains begin to mirror one another.[15] As a result, as time goes on, we begin to act more like that other person.[16]

you're intentional about creating the right environment for your dreams.

If anyone you've surrounded yourself with becomes too negative, you need to remove them from your Starting Five. The last thing you want to do is have toxic people on the journey with you. I've had to make the tough decision to distance myself from certain individuals who didn't bring me closer to my dreams. The people you want in the game with you are the ones who support your dreams. The one thing that members of my Starting Five always have in common is this: When life gets tough, I don't need to look for them. I know they have my back.

So who are your Starting Five? Of course, you don't have to have exactly five people in your inner circle, but you will want to keep that circle pretty small to stay closely connected. Up to this point, the people you've spent the most time with may have simply come together by accident. Most dreamers will need to adjust their Starting Five as they grow. Not only is that okay, it is also absolutely necessary for creating an environment in which your dreams can thrive.

When Cindy and I started flipping houses, I read every book and talked to every person I could about the subject. I became mildly obsessed with gathering the knowledge I needed to succeed. But I noticed that the people who were in my Starting Five back then talked more about sports or what they watched on television. There's nothing wrong with that, of course, but I needed to find people who shared my interests or who were willing to share their expertise with me. I stayed friends with a lot of those people, but at any given time, only a select handful were members of my Starting Five.

If your dreams don't have the support of a healthy Starting Five, they'll wither and die. I'm giving you permission right now to get intentional about who influences you so you can create an environment in which your dreams will thrive.

THE INFLUENCE MATRIX

People make all the difference. Period. If you surround yourself with the right influencers, the sky's the limit.

After reflecting on my experience with people over the years, I created what I call the Influence Matrix to help evaluate the relationships you need to be part of your Starting Five. It's a simple tool you can use to decide if you should protect your dreams from someone or add them to your inner circle to help you move those dreams forward.

As you can see in the following illustration, the Influence Matrix builds off the intersection of two things: whether the person has done what you want to do or not *and* whether they are discouraging or encouraging to you along the way. These guidelines create four distinct quadrants in which each of the four types of people live.

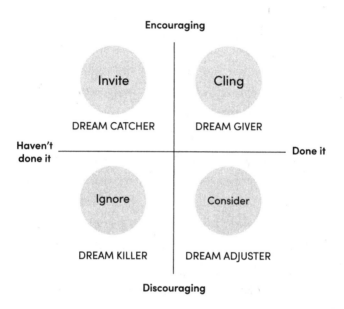

My Starting Five list presently includes several people who are Dream Catchers, one Dream Adjuster, and one Dream Giver. And *no one* who is a Dream Killer. Here's a description of each type:

The Dream Catcher. This person encourages you as you pursue your dreams, but they don't have as much experience doing what you want to do. Whatever you do, don't discard these people from your life simply because they haven't done what you want to do.

You can think of Dream Catchers as your cheerleaders. You want these people in your life to lift your spirits on those days when you need a pat on the back, even though they don't have the skill set to play the game you want to play—at least not yet. With the right can-do attitude, they may be able to jump in and help figure it out, like Steve has done so many times for me.

That is why I suggest the action you take with these people is this: *invite* them to join you. If it is possible for them to get in the game alongside you, that's great! If not, enlist their help as cheerleaders to keep the fire of your passion lit when the going gets tough. My confidant, Chris, serves as another Dream Catcher for me by encouraging me and giving me a safe place to talk through challenges.

Often these people can be peers who are on a similar dream journey. As I reflect on my own experience, those people were often other up-and-coming talents—coaches, entrepreneurs, salespeople, or business leaders—who shared elements of my own dream. Because we were in similar stages, we could compare notes and push each other to reach further when either of us felt discouraged.

I saw this role brought to life in the movie *The Intern* with Anne Hathaway and Robert DeNiro. A retired executive, played by DeNiro, decides to leave his life of leisure and get back in the game by becoming an intern at Hathaway's e-commerce company. Hathaway's character is a young entrepreneur who has good ideas but lacks the confidence to really take charge. Because of his previous experiences, DeNiro becomes the Dream Catcher Hathaway needs to encourage her to come into her own as a leader.

Like you, these people don't know what they don't know, but they are eager to find out and share what they learn. Plus, on those days when your belief levels dip, they'll be there to let you borrow their belief, and vice versa.

The Dream Adjuster. This individual has experience related to what you want to do. They either had success doing it and know a lot, or they didn't have success and learned a lot. But for whatever reason, they believe you should adjust your approach if you want to succeed.

Their input can be critical to help you identify pitfalls or gaps to avoid in your plan.

Perhaps that person succeeded at what you want to do and now knows a better, more effective way for you to achieve your dreams. If someone said to me today, "Mark, I want to start a health-oriented business like you did," I'd have a ready-made list of what-not-to-dos based on my own experiences.

However, if you're not careful, input from a Dream Adjuster can be overwhelming and make you want to quit. Sometimes these well-meaning people can get bogged down in the details because they ask a lot of *how* questions to make sure everything lines up: *How are you going to do that? How will you get this done? How exactly do you plan to solve that issue?* Those are good questions to ask, but an over-emphasis on them can also be negative for you and your team. So be careful how much exposure you have to Dream Adjusters who have that effect on you. No matter their intentions, you don't need any extra temptation to quit.

The best thing to do with Dream Adjusters is to ask *them* a lot of questions. At the very least, learn from their experiences. You may just find that you *do* need to adjust your dream in a healthy way based on their input. You may learn that you still want the same dream, but you need to approach it in a different way.

The best action to take when you encounter a Dream Adjuster is this: Carefully *consider* what they have to say. Then make your own decision. Think of their input as potentially valuable advice to heed or a negative voice to ignore—but *not* the final word on your dreams.

The Dream Givers. These people should be your main influencers, the kind of people you always want in your inner circle. Not only have they done what you want to do, they are also encouraging you and are willing to help you get where you want to go. Keith has been this person for me so many times over the years. His expert guidance has given my dreams energy and life they otherwise would not have had.

We've had so many Dream Givers along our dream journey that to try to name all of them would most likely fill an entire book. We're so incredibly grateful to all our Dream Givers who have come in and out of our lives along the way. During those seasons when they were with us, we leaned into their wisdom as much as we possibly could.

I encourage you to do the same thing. When you find a Dream Giver, there is only one thing to do if they will let you: *Cling* to them. Don't let them go without learning from them.

Keep in mind that people in this quadrant are often successful, so their time may be limited. Always be careful to respect that fact as you ask for their input.

Then be prepared to act based on their input. No one wants to invest time trying to teach someone who doesn't listen. Don't be that person. Ask. Listen. Learn. Don't let go—and watch yourself grow.

The Dream Killer. These people have never done what you want to do, but they still actively discourage you from trying to follow your dreams. When it comes to discussing your dreams, they should be avoided at all costs. You do not want these people on your Starting Five—or anywhere near you if you can help it.

We all have potential Dream Killers in our lives. Unfortunately, they're often close family members or longtime friends. I try to give these people the benefit of the doubt. They likely care about you and don't want to see you experience the pain of failure. They may think they're helping you by discouraging you from trying for more. On the other hand, they may just be too stuck in their own fears.

I can't count how many times people have come up to me after opportunity meetings about It Works! and told me how excited they are to join the team. Then one day later, they come back and we have a conversation that goes something like this:

"Mr. Pentecost, this seems like such a great opportunity and everything I've been looking for, but . . . my Uncle Joe says it will never work and that I shouldn't join."

"Well, it's certainly good to be cautious," I assure them, "but I'm living proof that it can work. By the way," I ask, "what does Uncle Joe do for a living?"

"He drives a school bus."

"Oh. Has he ever built a business or done anything like this before?"

"No."

"I see," I try to reply as tactfully as I can. "Nothing against your uncle, but I wouldn't go to a mechanic to find out about brain surgery, and I'm not going to a brain surgeon to find out about fixing my car."

I have found that everyone has an Uncle Joe in their lives. If you're not careful, their negativity can derail you right from the start. When you find a Dream Killer, I suggest you take this action: *Ignore* them. That's right. You don't have to be a jerk about it, but set boundaries so they know your dreams are not up for debate. Plus, you'll have to decide how much you'll share your plans with them to avoid getting discouraged by their negative opinions.

It's not only the obviously negative or fearful people who will kill your dreams. Even people who initially seem to be on your side can turn toxic. In the days before we started It Works!, we experienced another environment with a highly competitive culture that became all about making money for the sake of making money. In that situation, the culture itself became a Dream Killer. We had to move on to keep our dreams alive.

We've worked to make sure a toxic environment didn't take hold at It Works! by making sure we put together a team of people who focus on building relationships and lifting each other up. That doesn't mean we don't have a competitive spirit. In fact, we love healthy competition. I've always been driven by the thrill of going for the win. Yet life is about more than driving harder and going faster than you did yesterday.

Toxic people create a toxic culture that can suck all the joy out of your dream journey. If you find yourself in a toxic environment, look for the exit as quickly as possible—and don't take any of that toxicity with you!

The makeup of your Starting Five can adjust to meet your needs, but be careful when including Dream Adjusters. Plus, always try to have at least one Dream Giver on your team. Each person thrives in the role that suits them best. If you try to force a Dream Catcher into the Dream Giver role, you'll be disappointed. Likewise, if you try to make a Dream Adjuster be your Dream Catcher, you may soon find yourself drained but not know why. When you let each person do what they naturally do best, you'll get the most value from the relationship and will position your dreams to thrive.

BUILDING YOUR BEST TEAM

If you need to build a team to grow your dreams in a business or other organization, the Influence Matrix can help. In addition to helping you identify members of your Starting Five, it can be used to evaluate members of any team.

First, the obvious: *no Dream Killers.* No team needs them for any reason. You don't have time for people who have no experience doing what you want and who discourage everyone around them. Don't hire them. And don't keep around anyone who turns into a Dream Killer.

Every team needs Dream Catchers to be willing to jump in and get things done and keep morale high.

These people will likely make up the majority of a growing team as you hunger for more and celebrate wins together. The neat thing about Dream Catchers is that their energy and enthusiasm act as catalysts to make everyone around them better.

As I mentioned, be cautious about how many Dream Adjusters you invite onto your team. Don't get me wrong—you need people who are willing to say no and question the status quo. But Dream Adjusters can be negative because of their own bad experiences. So be careful when adding them to your team. If they are more discouraging than encouraging, move on from them.

Finally, the Dream Givers are key to helping any team grow beyond what they know right now. When trying anything new, there is so much you don't even know that you need to know. You always need Dream Givers—or at least access to them—for your team to go to the next level. A Dream Giver gives your entire team a critical shortcut to success.

Unfortunately, Dream Givers can be challenging to find, both for your Starting Five and if you are building a team. One practice that has worked well for me is simply to engage with people doing life around me. After we moved to our new house back in Grand Rapids, I played three-on-three basketball games with other guys in our neighborhood. As I got to know more about each of their areas of expertise, I soon discovered many were business owners and leaders with a lot more experience than I had then. So I leaned in to their expertise.

I play a lot of pickleball games now to connect with other people. As we play, I get to know more about what each of the other players brings to the table. Your interests will be different, of course, but seek out people who share them—chat with your neighbors at the local coffee shop, engage with folks in your favorite online forums, or talk with members of your church or local business association.

Ask yourself these questions to help you find those important Dream Givers:

> **HUDDLE UP!**
>
> I'm a people person, so I'm always going to seek out in-person influencers first. If you don't have someone to connect with yet, check out podcasts, online videos, social media, audiobooks, and helpful books like this one to find the people who've done what you want to do. Not only will this expand your knowledge base and give you new ideas about how to make your dream a reality, but when you find your real-life mentors, you'll be able to get to the deeper conversations faster and have something you can give back to them.

- *What knowledge or expertise do I need for the next season of my dream journey?* Figure out what you don't know that you need to know. Identify your greatest knowledge gaps. As you progress and experience growth, think about what might "break" next.

- *Who do I know who has what I need?* Start by thinking through your existing network. Expand from there to brainstorming possible other sources. Ask people you respect if they know of people who might provide what you need. It might even help to put it out there on social media: "When it comes to [the expertise you need], who are the most knowledgeable people you know?"

- *How can I add value to them?* If you are asking for help from someone you don't know well (or at all), start by finding a way to add value to them. It may be as simple as sharing a link to a helpful resource they mentioned online. It may involve volunteering your time or energy to be of help to them in some way or making connections for them. Consider offering to treat them to lunch or a cup of coffee. Whatever it may be in your situation, approaching them with a *giving* posture will best position you to connect in a deeper, more meaningful way.

- *Am I ready to receive their help?* Don't be afraid to receive help from people during this season of growth. There will always be seasons of giving and receiving in any relationship. Some people struggle to accept help from others, even when they really need it, so make sure you're open to guidance before you ask for it. What a Dream Giver says may go against what you currently think. You may need to lay down your ego to let them lift you up.

- *What is the best way to approach them to ask for their guidance?* Every situation will be unique, so be ready to stay flexible. In general, most influencers respond favorably when you share a compelling vision for your dream, a willingness to do the work needed to succeed, and a learner's attitude. If they are not available, thank them for their time and ask if they can recommend someone else who might be a better fit to help you.

When you use the Influence Matrix to help you choose who you let into your life, you intentionally cultivate an environment in which your dreams can thrive. Be intentional about seeking Dream Catchers, Dream Adjusters, and Dream Givers while ignoring those Dream Killers. You'll be well on your way to putting your absolute best Starting Five on the court for every season of your dream journey. Soon, you'll be ready to celebrate your wins!

YOUR DREAM PLAN

1. **Your Starting Five:** It matters who runs beside you as you chase your dream. Surround yourself with people who motivate you to keep moving toward it. You need people who inspire you, increase your resilience, and cheer you on to get back up.

   - Think about the key people in your life right now. Who would you say is on your Starting Five? (Remember, you can have more or fewer than five.)

   - What is it about their characteristics, values, or experience that stands out to you?

2. **The Influence Matrix:**

   - Have you ever encountered a **Dream Killer**—someone who has never done what you want to do *and* who discourages you from reaching for more?

— What did they say to you, and how did it make you feel?

— Why do you think they discouraged you?

— Do you need to create some distance between yourself and any Dream Killers in your life right now?

- Who are the **Dream Catchers** in your life right now—the ones who cheer you on despite never having done what you've set out to do?

— In what specific ways has a Dream Catcher encouraged you?

— How can you invite that person to join your dream journey?

- Think about any **Dream Adjusters** you may have encountered—people who have some experience doing what you want to do but who have discouraged you from going after it in the way you intended.

  — What did they say to you?

  — Why do you think they discouraged you?

  — What can you learn from their experience?

- Who are some possible **Dream Givers** who have done what you want to do and might be willing to guide you?

  — What do they say or do that fuels your desire to achieve?

  — How can you thank them for their help or example?

— If possible, meet with them or have a meal together. Ask the tough questions, and get every nugget of advice you need. Remember to treat them to dessert!

3. **Influencers You Haven't Met—Yet:** Think of the people who might influence you but whom you haven't met. They may have inspired you by their story as you listened to them on a podcast, followed them on social media, or read their book.

- How have they already influenced you?

- Think of ways you can learn more from those people. Do they have a podcast or video channel? Subscribe to it. Have they written a book about your dream topic? Read it. Do they offer an online course or a life seminar? Take it.

Celebrate Your Wins

*Celebrations should happen at
milestones, not just destinations.*

Our twenty-year anniversary celebration for It Works! was unlike anything I had ever experienced. After COVID had kept us separated for so long, we had to wait for the opportunity to come together, but it was worth it. Our ultimate party that night did not disappoint.

We put up a huge tent with a stage right there on our ranch in Florida. We invited not only our company team members but also personal friends and others who had supported us over the years. We planned and paid for the party to *wow* everyone, but even I was blown away by the black-tie affair. It was first-class all the way.

As photographers snapped pictures, we entered on a red carpet through dazzling tunnels of twinkling lights—just as the sun was preparing to set. Glittering gold balls hung above, making it feel as if the entire tent were sparkling. We had our own It Works! Walk of Fame to honor people who were part of the company's success. In addition to a delicious catered dinner, we featured a cigar-making station where anyone who wanted to could hand-wrap a celebratory cigar. My team even had a surprise for me: They planned special drinks that somehow featured my own face (yes, me, Mark Pentecost) smiling up at everyone from the top of the foam. I never thought I'd see anything like that! We held nothing back that night.

We kicked off the night with an awards ceremony where we invited people onstage to thank them publicly for all they had done. Then, just when everyone thought the night couldn't possibly get better, the curtains behind us on the stage pulled back to reveal Little Big Town! That's right, we brought a *Grammy Award–winning country music band* to party with us.

The energetic concert experience blew everyone away. We sang, danced, partied, and just had a blast! But we weren't done yet. We took the celebration to *a whole 'notha level* by lighting up the night sky with a stunning fireworks display! The dazzling bursts of light and thundering booms simply took my breath away.

Just as the fireworks finished and everyone thought the night might be over, a jazz band from Texas started playing at the other end of the massive tent. The dance floor was open! No one wanted to leave as we all partied well into that memorable night.

The entire event was so special that it felt like a scene from a movie. I had always dreamed of hosting an ultimate celebration like that one, but to be honest, it surpassed even my own expectations. I'd really dreamed big on behalf of all the people who had helped us on our dream journey. I wanted the night to be one they would remember for a lifetime. It was our biggest celebration yet, and I can't wait for the next one. I'm looking forward to inviting dreamers like *you* to it.

Our celebrations have certainly grown alongside our dreams, but early on, we embraced this game-changing truth: Don't wait until you reach your ultimate dream destination to celebrate. Celebrate at every milestone along the way.

THE CELEBRATION HABIT LOOP

I want to make sure you enjoy your dream journey as much as I've enjoyed mine. That night was the ultimate party, but imagine after all these years if that were the only celebration I could talk about. That wouldn't be fun at all. We didn't wait to celebrate until we could throw that incredible party; we made a habit of celebrating milestones as a family or as a team all along the way, creating some of my happiest memories.

Cindy and I always instinctively celebrated every dream achievement because we were so excited that we'd actually done it. We didn't wait until we had reached our ultimate dream destination. Whenever we flipped and sold a house, we'd go out for steak and lobster. Trust me, on a teacher's salary, that was a luxury we usually couldn't afford. I thought I had arrived!

Celebrating helps create momentum for achieving your dreams and develops positive memories you can call on for future motivation. That's why it's so powerful to celebrate each win—it keeps you invested in your long-term dreams.

What Cindy and I didn't realize at the time was that every time we celebrated, we were rewiring our brains with reward circuits that motivated us to keep going. Every time you celebrate an accomplishment— no matter how small it may seem—it releases all the feel-good hormones in your brain: serotonin, oxytocin, dopamine, and endorphins.[17] When this happens, your mind subconsciously connects what you just did with feeling awesome, which makes you want to do that thing again. So, quite literally, the more you dream, achieve that dream, and celebrate your accomplishment, the more you will want to dream. You can literally train yourself to dream and achieve with the Celebration Habit Loop.

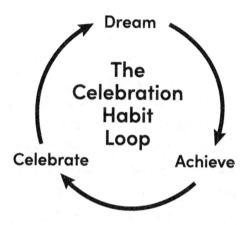

Here's even better news: It won't take long to make celebration a habit. The latest research by Stanford psychologist B. J. Fogg suggests that the act of celebrating itself can do the trick. "Sometimes, all you need," Fogg says, "is a shot of positive feeling and emotion, a dose of celebration" to reinforce micro changes, or "tiny habits," as he calls them, that make big successes possible.[18]

In case you hadn't noticed, we live in a world that tends to be pretty negative. You'll probably need to condition yourself to celebrate, just like with the workouts you give your Dream Muscle. That's why it's so important to make celebration a habit that you don't even need to think about—just do it!

Let's walk through each of the three components of the Celebration Habit Loop to make sure you can tap into this simple but powerful practice:

1. **Dream.** This entire book is about dreaming, of course, but you need to focus on a specific goal in order to connect it with a celebration. If there is no clarity about the goal, there can never be anything to celebrate. It sounds obvious, but often the reason so many people fail to celebrate is they don't know *what* to celebrate. They've never set clear goals in the first place. You can use the Dream Script you created earlier as your starting point. But remember that celebrations happen at milestones, not just destinations, so break down large goals into manageable milestones so you can celebrate as you go. Our twentieth anniversary party was amazing, but we celebrated often throughout the journey to get there. Don't wait until you can throw the ultimate party when you reach your ultimate destination.

2. **Achieve.** Next, you need a plan to achieve those goals. We didn't leave the success of It Works! to chance or rely on hope as our strategy. We

developed a plan we believed could get us there, and then we poured energy and effort into making it happen. Without a plan, the likelihood of you ever getting to celebrate goes down a lot. But a powerful plan is a path to a party!

Make sure your plan includes milestones that matter. This is key: You actually need to accomplish the goal for that milestone before you can celebrate. It's a reward for your effort, not a participation trophy for showing up. Just knowing the celebration is coming when you achieve the goal helps keep everyone motivated and engaged.

Another advantage to setting meaningful milestones is that it helps people see tangible progress toward a larger goal. It can be easy to lose focus if your dream goal takes a while. Celebrating when you achieve each step along the way keeps everyone energized about what they are doing now.

3. **Celebrate.** I want to have the energy and passion to party when I win! I want to celebrate with a fun end-zone dance! And I want the same for you. If you've ever seen a touchdown scored in a football game, you've probably seen a lot of variations of end-zone dance celebrations. Some are coordinated, some are solo, and some involve choreography and even backflips. I've seen

players bust some moves that would be impressive on any dance floor. The point is that the players celebrate in their own unique way. And the team and fans love it!

Do the same thing when *you* celebrate! Plan your end-zone dance ahead of time. What crazy moves will you make? Your dance doesn't have to include backflips, but make it your own. Visualize exactly how you will celebrate *when*—not *if*—you reach those milestones. Sure, there will be challenges to face and setbacks to overcome, but the habit of consistent celebrations keeps the focus on what fuels you. By celebrating at each milestone, you create a self-sustaining and self-motivating celebration loop.

When Cindy and I started out in that first direct-selling business, we built on our habit of lobster and steak dinners, and we put a trip to Hawaii—without the kids—on our Dream Board. We set a goal and planned to take that trip when we achieved it. It didn't take long. Now, we could have kept working, afraid that we might lose momentum by taking a break. But it was time to celebrate!

We had hardly ever flown anywhere because most of our vacations involved piling the kids into the van and driving to Florida for spring break. The

Hawaii trip was full of firsts, and, yes, you bet we spoiled ourselves! We stayed in a luxury hotel with a beautiful view of the Pacific Ocean.

With no kids jumping on the bed every morning, we slept in. We sipped coffee while looking over the blue sea, listening to the waves crashing on the beach. We ate freshly cut pineapple every day. Someone else made all our meals and washed all the dishes. We lay on reclining chairs by the pool and read books we never had the time to read before. We toured the islands and took long walks together. I played golf on some incredible courses while Cindy enjoyed being pampered at the spa. In short, we had a dream to achieve, we achieved it, and then we gave ourselves permission to celebrate and appreciate how far we'd come.

> ## HUDDLE UP!
>
> Bring your celebration to life with your own end-zone dance! It's a wild release of energy. Plus, it's just plain fun! Live a little on the wild side here and create your own moves. Turn on your favorite pump-it-up music and choreograph a dance that celebrates *you*! Bonus points if you record it. Share your end-zone dance on social media and tag #MarkPentecost and #DreamPhenomenon.

After you dream, celebrate milestones to drive you until you achieve that dream, and then celebrate that big win in style, what happens next? That big celebration motivates you to want to dream again—or (re)dream, as I call it. And the Celebration Habit Loop continues.

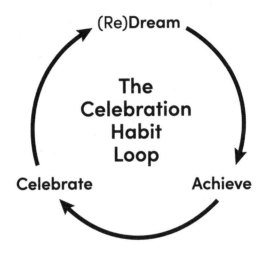

We'll explore redreaming more in the next chapter. First, I want to explore some key points about *how* to celebrate to maximize your motivation.

YOUR CELEBRATION CIRCLES

You'll connect with a lot of people who will help you on your journey to achieve your dreams. So when you celebrate, you don't at the party, alone with your cake and balloons. Instead, think about *how* you will celebrate with the people who've helped you succeed. I created Celebration Circles to remind me to be intentional about this. The Celebration Circles naturally start with you; however, as your dreams grow and involve more people, your celebrations should expand to include those people in the fun.

> ## HUDDLE UP!
>
> Pull out your Dream Board! Just as Cindy and I put our dream vacation to Hawaii on our board, take a minute to think about how you're going to celebrate when you achieve your next dream. It might be something like a dinner out at that restaurant you've always wanted to try or a day at the spa for that massage you've always wanted to get. Just make sure it's something you don't do every day and that it fills you up. Then go ahead and put it on your Dream Board!

Here's how the Celebration Circles work:

Circle 1: You. Take the time to enjoy *your* own success. This is your dream, after all. Don't be afraid to do a little self-care to reward yourself for a job well done. Don't fall into the trap of thinking you're only as good as your next win.

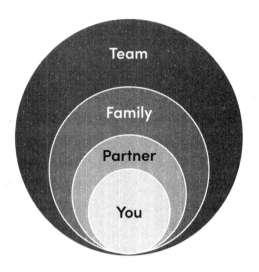

No wins are too small to celebrate, so take the time to celebrate *each* of them.

One of my favorite ways to celebrate is to get out on the golf course and play the game I love. I enjoy that mix of relaxation and challenge, especially when I can golf with friends who share my competitive drive. I enjoy giving it my best in friendly competition and spending time with the people who fill me up. I find it helps me reset, reflect, and get ready for the next thing. I do the same with pickleball and even chess. If I know I have a challenging day or week ahead, I schedule one of these activities to give myself something to look forward to when I achieve my goal.

You might treat yourself to a nice lunch, get a massage, buy a new outfit, spend time in nature, or whatever it is that is meaningful for you. Do what recharges you to celebrate wins and inspires you to take the next step in your dream journey.

Circle 2: Partner. Think about how you will celebrate with your partner or significant other. When Cindy and I hit our milestones, we always celebrate together with date nights or even something big like that Hawaii trip. However, Cindy likes to celebrate differently than I do. For one thing, she doesn't like to play golf. She prefers a dinner out or some other experience we can enjoy together. A lot of times, she also likes gathering the family—kids and grandkids alike—to celebrate successes with those who mean the most to her.

I suspect your partner or significant other may like celebrating differently than you do. How do they like to celebrate? This might make a great date-night question to ask next time you are out.

If your partner likes flowers—and especially if they did something to help you hit that milestone—send them flowers to celebrate. Take them out to their favorite restaurant for dinner. Get tickets to that show *they've* been wanting to see or to that sporting event *they've* been wanting to attend.

On the other hand, maybe you have a partner who seems reluctant to support your dreams. When that happens, you may want to "salt the oats," as my grandfather put it. He liked to say that you can't make a horse drink, but if you salt the oats, they'll get thirsty—and gladly drink on their own. I've seen this happen many times with reluctant partners. My best advice is to learn how they like to celebrate. The next time you hit a milestone, "salt the oats" by including your partner, and celebrate in a style that speaks to them.

As they begin to enjoy the rewards—flowers, jewelry, events, experiences, or whatever it might be—they'll see that what you're doing is not only good for you but also good for them. They may even want to start helping you achieve more of your dreams!

Circle 3: Family. My family is always foremost in my mind, so it was vital that our kids felt like they were part of our dreams too. Even when they were young, we held family meetings before we started working toward a big goal or milestone. We told the kids that Mom and Dad were going to be working hard for a period of time, and we asked for their support to help us reach our destination. Then we talked about how we would all celebrate as a family when we reached the goal. If we made a certain amount in sales, we might go out for pizza and mini golf.

In this way, we taught them not only that Mom and Dad worked for the benefit of the family but also that it is important to celebrate wins. Additionally, they were learning that, as part of the family, they contributed to our overall success. We were one team. And just like with those Dream Boards, they now teach their own kids to celebrate together.

Maybe you feel it's silly to include your kids in the celebration. After all, they're just kids. They should know that parents need to work. Maybe that was your experience as a child, but if you're always working for the family and never include them in the celebration, they might not make the connections between your work and the rewards. Instead, they'll just remember how much you were gone or how many games or recitals you missed.

Including my kids made them feel like we were all on the dream journey together— because we were. For one thing, it set the expectation that they were important to me in the midst of busy seasons of life. As a result, even now my adult daughter Kindsey says she never remembers me missing special events such as games, recitals, or birthdays. Of course, I did have to miss some events from time to time, but because I brought them all into the journey with shared celebrations, she only remembers me being present.

By keeping them in the Celebration Circles, you can help your family see the purpose behind the work and allow them to contribute. Celebrating together strengthens your family for generations to come and helps make dreamers of them all.

Circle 4: Team. Last, but certainly not least, celebrate with your team—in a way they would enjoy. When I say "your team," I mean anyone who helps you bring your dream to life. Your team will go further when you celebrate in a way that resonates with them. They simply can't sustain an endless pattern of dream-achieve-re-dream-achieve. They need to pause and celebrate the wins in a way that matters to them.

I mentioned that I love to celebrate by golfing. So did my team. If we had a few good weeks, we'd shut down the office for an afternoon and head to our golf course. The main objective was simply to have fun in the sun together. We did other things, too, but the point was we worked hard as a team, so we celebrated as a team—and in a way that mattered to them.

Many years later, I still have team members tell me how much those impromptu celebrations meant to them. By showing people you appreciate them as you create positive memories together, you give them the fuel they need to continue the dream journey—and have fun doing it!

It's easy to focus on how you want to celebrate and forget about how everyone else may want to celebrate. So, who is in your Celebration Circles? Do you know how you like to celebrate or how that aligns with your partner? What about your family? Do they know they are part of the journey and the celebration planning too? As for your team, when was the last time you celebrated with them? Have you ever asked team members how they want to celebrate and what type of celebration is meaningful to them? If you don't already know the answers to those questions, it sounds like you've got some fun to plan!

CELEBRATE IN STYLE

Some people struggle to celebrate. Maybe you grew up in a house where you didn't see anyone else celebrate wins. Maybe you feel like you've never had a reason to celebrate in the past. Perhaps you tend to be so driven that you always focus on your next goal instead of taking the time to celebrate. Believe me, I get it.

But what happens when you don't take time to celebrate? *Burnout.* If you don't celebrate the wins along the way, you drain your mental and emotional tank. When you run out of steam to enjoy life, your drive to achieve your dreams eventually slows down.

I confess it's always been a little challenging for me to really rest in celebration moments. Because I love everything I do, work has never felt like work to me. I could work eight days in a row without thinking twice about it. After achieving one goal, I tend to celebrate for a minute, then focus on the next goal—without giving myself time to fully enjoy the celebration. I've had to condition myself not only to celebrate but also to enjoy leaning in to that time of celebration.

What wins might be happening around you right now that you're not celebrating? It's easy to forget that we all need to pause and pat ourselves on the back occasionally. Even if you're only celebrating that you turned in a report on time, kept your workout commitment, or were fully present with your kids after dinner—those are all wins!

Another consequence of not taking the time to celebrate is the damage of *stress*. If you're constantly in work or achievement mode, you damage your physical and mental health. Coming out of the COVID-19 pandemic in 2020, I think we all became more aware of the dangers of chronic stress. It can cause headaches, insomnia, fatigue, chest pains, and a weakened immune system—as well as anxiety, restlessness, lack of focus or motivation, anger, depression, and a sense of overwhelm. If any of those sound like your own life experience, I urge you to pay attention to the warning signs.

Your dreams need you to be fully present and as healthy as possible to bring them to life. Your health and relationships depend on you taking time to enjoy the journey and be fully present as you celebrate every milestone.

To avoid both burnout and stress, I suggest three key celebration practices:

1. **Find your celebration style.** Each person has a little different definition of what it means to celebrate. Some people like to hang out with a lot of friends and throw a party. Others may want to have a quiet dinner with a couple of close

companions. Don't try to fit into someone else's celebration box; find what works best for you. If it fills you up and matters to you, it will work. However, don't forget to think about the Celebration Circles and how your family or team may want to celebrate. What works for you may not work for them.

2. **Be fully present.** Like I said, I'm always excited about what's next, so I have to intentionally leave my phone or other distractions behind and celebrate just like I planned. It's so easy to be "in the room" but not engaged with the celebration. Give yourself permission to pause and lean into those celebration times. Silence your notifications or set your phone aside entirely to ensure you're fully present in those moments. Don't just check the box of celebrating; live in the moment and enjoy it!

3. **Condition yourself to celebrate daily.** The little wins are the easiest to overlook. But when you make celebrating a daily practice, you condition yourself to see the progress you make every single day. Did you work out today? *Celebrate that!* Did you hug your children after they finished breakfast? *Well done!* Did you make the calls you intended to make or complete a key task today? *Woohoo!* Congratulate yourself for

doing what you committed to do—and you'll be positioned to do even more tomorrow.

By celebrating each win, you increase your awareness of just how much there is to celebrate in your life. Every day, you condition yourself to celebrate a little more. As an extra perk, researchers have found that celebrating your successes consistently builds your self-esteem and confidence,[19] which then increase your ability to dream.

I get excited thinking about all the fun you'll have celebrating as you achieve your milestone wins along the way. As you do, you'll create incredible memories with those you love. Plus—and this is huge—your celebration habit will propel you and your dreams to *a whole 'notha level!*

YOUR DREAM PLAN

1. **What will you celebrate?** Think about your dream and the path to accomplish it. Rather than waiting until you reach your ultimate destination, are there natural milestones along the way at which you can celebrate your progress?

   - What milestone celebration could you plan in the next thirty, sixty, or ninety days?

   - Think about school schedules, family visits, birthdays, or holidays. When can you schedule time to celebrate your next win? Are there certain days or times that work better than others?

2. **Who will you celebrate with?**
   - How do you like to celebrate? Give yourself permission to celebrate in ways that fill you up.

   - How does your partner like to celebrate? How does this differ from your own celebration style? How might you celebrate the next win in a way that will be meaningful to them?

- How does your family like to celebrate? What celebrations would your family enjoy as you develop a positive association with the time you invest into your dream journey?

- How does your team like to celebrate? What fun ways can you celebrate with your team and show your appreciation that will be meaningful to them?

3. **How will you celebrate?**
   - What is your celebration style? What sounds fun to you? Celebrate in ways that are *life-giving* and not simply an escape from daily life.

     — What activities best offer you a chance to recharge your battery?

— What locations offer you a peaceful chance to refocus your mind for what's next?

— How can you leverage those to honor what you've done so far?

- What is one key thing you can do to make sure you are fully present for your next celebration?

- What micro-celebrations can you do on a daily basis as you achieve wins each day?

Dare to Redream

*The dream that will make you most proud
is the one you're afraid to say out loud.*

By 2012, It Works! had been headquartered in Florida for a few years. We had achieved an unbelievable level of success that I struggled to fully grasp. In fact, that year we started hitting sales numbers like never before and reached $40 million in annual revenue!

As a former coach and teacher from a blue-collar family who first dared to dream about having more cash than bills, it would've been easy to fall into the "Blockbuster" mindset. I could have thought, *I'm doing just fine. I don't need to redream.* But that's precisely when you must.

I admit that I felt pretty good about our success. That year, the owners of *Direct Selling News* invited me to attend their annual conference, which included a banquet and awards for the Top 100 direct-selling companies. Every year since the founding of It Works!, I had declined the invitation. I didn't think I could afford to step away from work, and I thought we were too small for events like that. However, now that we were achieving such big numbers, I felt like we finally deserved to be there.

We met some amazing leaders and business owners at the event, as everyone graciously shared their experiences and industry knowledge. But the most eye-opening moment of the weekend came during the awards banquet. I was feeling good about our latest sales accomplishments—until they started naming the Top 100 companies. I thought for sure we had made the list until I discovered that all the companies on the Top 100 list had an annual revenue of *at least* $100 million. We only had $40 million.

Frustrated, I excused myself from the table and went to stand by the back wall. While I was standing there thinking, a man came up and stood next to me, but I didn't even notice him until he said, "You don't look very happy."

"I'm not," I replied, not really wanting to talk. "I don't like being so far out of the Top 100. We've got a long way to go." As happy as I'd been when I'd arrived at the conference, I could feel something stirring within me once again. I found myself dreaming of walking across that stage next year as part of the Top 100. *It was time to redream.*

For the rest of the conference, the seed of that next dream began to grow. I just *knew* we had the potential to make that list the next year. We would need to grow at least two and half times. But we were a team of dreamers.

I have to confess that I was initially a little afraid to voice my redream out loud when I got back to Florida. But on Monday morning, I entered the office fired up and ready to go, and I called a leadership meeting.

"Team, I have seen what's next for us," I announced. Their faces showed a mix of excitement and curiosity about what that might be. "Our goal is to make the Top 100 list next year."

Someone asked, "What do we need to be on the list?"

"At least $100 million in annual revenue."

Someone else half-joked, "Oh, $100 million. Is that all?"

We all shared a laugh, and then I added, "I know it sounds like a lot, but we went from almost having to close our doors to making $40 million a year in just a few years. We know how to do it. It won't be easy, but after all we've been through, I *know* we can do this!"

By the end of the meeting, we had created a slogan communicating the plan to everyone: *One Team, One Mission, One Hundred Million.* A new dream had begun. It was time to Get in the Game.

After we introduced the new dream to the rest of the It Works! family, we followed the Dream Phenomenon steps to achieve it:

- We put the slogan everywhere (step 2: Say It and See It).
- We took the necessary risks to go after such a big dream (step 3: Live on Offense).
- We re-strategized when things didn't go as planned (step 4: Get Back Up).
- We added some key players to the team (step 5: Find Your People).
- We celebrated every step of the way (step 6: Celebrate Your Wins).

By the very next year, we not only made the Top 100 List, we hit number twenty-seven! We also won the fastest-growing company award, earned a spot on the Inc. 500, and received a special leadership award. That's the power of what I call redreaming!

THE DREAM THAT WILL MAKE
YOU MOST PROUD

Every dream I've ever had started out as the Dream to End All Dreams, at least for that season of my life. But, as you've seen, each time I achieved that "ultimate" dream, I didn't stop there. A new dream always took its place—one that I hadn't dared to believe was possible before.

It all goes back to this reality: the day you start dreaming is the day you start living. If you're still breathing, there's still time for dreaming. It's what you were born to do. So when you achieve one dream and the celebration is done, it's time to Dare to Redream.

I call this the final step in the

> **HUDDLE UP!**
>
> Make your own slogan that captures the essence of your dream. You can even invite your family and team members to help you create it. If you really want to have some creative fun, take it a step further and design your own sign, flag, or banner to hang where you can see it every day. Then share a picture of your slogan on your favorite social media accounts. Don't forget to tag #DreamPhenomenon and #MarkPentecost to connect with the Dreamer community!

Dream Phenomenon, but it's really about restarting the dream cycle—only at *a whole 'notha level*. You see, your first dream (the one I hope you wrote down earlier) is a Good Dream. Like with my own first dream, when you wrote it down, it may have felt like the Dream to End All Dreams. However, as you achieve that dream—or even before you do—you'll likely find yourself daring to dream a little more. That's not to dismiss your first dream—not at all. You simply want to continue to listen to that stirring within and give your dreaming capacity room to grow as you do. Once you've redreamed a few times, the process begins to happen automatically without you needing to think about doing it—a lot like breathing.

Daring to redream is vital to realizing your dreams. If you don't believe me, ask Blockbuster. I know, some of you are wondering what Blockbuster is—and for good reason. In the 1990s and early 2000s (maybe even before you were born), their stores were everywhere. This was before DVDs became popular, and online streaming hadn't yet been invented. We "streamed" our movies by heading to a Blockbuster store on a Friday night, hoping to find the latest new release on the shelves. Of course, we had to return the movies by Monday morning or pay a fine. Trust me, it was a pain, but it was all we had—until Netflix entered the market.

Now that's a name you know, right? Here's why: Netflix offered to sell its business to Blockbuster at the height of video-tape popularity, but Blockbuster had a problem. Their first dream had succeeded so well that they stopped dreaming, and, consequently, they stopped growing. In short, their leaders had forgotten how to redream. Can you believe their CEO even said that online businesses would not be sustainable and would never make money? They got stuck in what had worked in the past—their brick-and-mortar retail stores—and passed on the opportunity to reimagine a faster, more convenient digital future. As a result, there is only one Blockbuster store remaining (it's located in Bend, Oregon), and Netflix rules the digital content world.

HUDDLE UP!

Do you tend to think one and done, or are you already eyeing your next dream? Maybe you have one or two dreams that really scare you—the ones you're afraid to say out loud. Let me tell you, those are the ones that will really make you proud when you see them come to life! So don't be afraid to go there. Write them down and tell yourself what they are. Then, if you have cheerleaders who support you in your dream journey, consider sharing those dreams with them to get some encouragement to redream again and again.

On the one hand, I get it. It's easy to get comfortable, and it can be a little scary to redream. It's easier to let your Dream Muscle rest and stop taking Good Risks than it is to pursue a better life for you and those you love. But let me assure you of one thing I know to be true about redreaming: The dreams that will make you most proud are the ones you're afraid to say out loud.

Dreaming has become a way of life for me. And, with a little nudge and practice, the same can be true for you as you take your dreams to *a whole 'notha level!*

A Whole 'Notha Level!

As you may have noticed, I like to use that expression a lot: *a whole 'notha level!* (But you've got to say it with passion and attitude!) I say it because I believe you can *always* dream more. In fact, I've found that, as you come to realize the power of redreaming, you can move through different levels of dreams, from Good to Great to Legendary.

> **Good Dreams** are your first dreams. You can't get anywhere until you get in the game and start achieving Good Dreams. Your first dreams are some of the most important ones

you'll ever have because they become the foundation for more dreams.

Our first dream of having more cash than bills was a Good Dream. In fact, you wouldn't be reading these words right now if it hadn't been for that dream. That first dream was scary to pursue, but it got us in the game. As we worked on it, we couldn't imagine anything beyond that dream because it was our Dream to End All Dreams. But once we accomplished it and experienced how good it felt to celebrate that hard work and achievement, it gave us an appetite for more, and we realized there was so much more to dream.

I have found that once you experience the power of dreaming, you get pretty eager to dream more. Once you reach your first dream and give yourself a chance to celebrate, you see the power of dreams and are inspired to keep moving forward.

Great Dreams stretch your belief levels and require more effort to achieve because they are often the ones you are afraid to say out loud. For Cindy and me, our first Great Dream was for me to leave teaching. When we finally dared to dream it after seeing a former basketball coach receive a huge check, we were initially afraid to tell anyone about that dream. We didn't know if we could do it or how long it would take to achieve. But we went after it with everything we had because we knew it would be a game-changing dream. Now we're proud that we took action.

As our Dream Muscles grew, another Great Dream was to move from small-town Allegan to Grand Rapids and buy a new lake house. Just a few years prior to that time, we couldn't see a way to do that. But we dared to dream a Great Dream. When we paid for that lake house in cash, we felt the relief of being debt-free.

With our Dream Muscles getting stronger every time, one of our next Great Dreams was starting It Works! That Great Dream would require more from us than ever before, and we had a lot to learn. We were breaking into an industry we'd never worked in before. We were importing the products ourselves. We were building a team from scratch. We were finding new customers in a completely new market. There were times when we didn't know if we'd make it, but we kept dreaming and punched through the potential barriers to business success.

When you have a Great Dream, you cannot stay who you are and get where you want to go. To break through the barrier, you must be willing to acknowledge what you don't know, let go of what you've already done, build the right team, and make sure you have the right people in the Influence Matrix. It *will* be uncomfortable. It *will* be challenging. But I guarantee the work will be worth it—not only for what you will achieve but also for the better person you will become in the process.

And do you know the most amazing thing about dreaming at this level? You realize not only that you can break through what you think is the ceiling but also that *there is no ceiling.* Talk about supercharging your dreams! Imagine what could be possible if we all learned to dream at *a whole 'notha level,* where the only limits were the ones we put on ourselves. What good might we all do in this world then?

The more we dreamed Great Dreams, the stronger our Dream Muscles became. Other Great Dreams involved giving back to causes we cared about, like supporting Dick Vitale's Cancer Heroes. We've sponsored several families with children going through cancer treatments and donated millions of dollars to the V Foundation and the Moffitt Cancer Center. We've also contributed millions to help rescue people enslaved by human trafficking. Those are all Great Dreams that we only dared to dream once we had seen the life-transforming power of dreaming.

When you feel a Great Dream stirring in your heart, don't let fear or resistance stop you from pursuing it. Often, that Great Dream will set you up to dare to dream at *a whole 'notha level*.

Legendary Dreams. As you dream more and more, you'll soon start dreaming Legendary Dreams—the ones that take dreaming to *a whole 'notha level!* They might even be dreams no one else has dared to dream before. Not only will you be afraid to say these dreams out loud, but they will cause your Dream Muscle to grow stronger than you ever imagined possible. They demand the most from you because

HUDDLE UP!

What might a Great Dream be for you? What dream are you thinking of, even now, that you are afraid to say out loud? I challenge you to go ahead and say it right now. That's right. Wherever you are, go ahead and say it. Then circle back to step 2 of the Dream Phenomenon and create a Dream Script for it so you can make it part of your dreaming habits.

they give the most to you—and touch many lives around you in the process.

For me, one of those dreams was breaking into that Top 100 list. Another was buying ten thousand acres for our cattle ranch in Florida. Owning a tropical island in the Caribbean certainly qualifies as one of our Legendary Dreams. All of these seemed mind-blowing and even a little crazy when we had them. All the best dreams do—until you achieve them. Then you realize you have been dreaming at—you guessed it—*a whole 'notha level!*

We definitely dreamed at *a whole 'notha level* when we filmed the feature film *Florida Wild* on our own cattle ranch. That Legendary Dream not only opened our eyes to what was possible on the ranch, but it also opened new dream pathways for us. Even now, we're dreaming about filming a few more movies and putting in a golf course on the ranch. That's what Legendary Dreams do—they open the floodgates for other dreams to pour in.

Now, you should know that we get pretty literal about dreaming at *a whole 'notha level.* When we built our three-story headquarters building right on the sparkling Manatee River near the Gulf of Mexico, we didn't just settle for good. We made the building *great* with an inviting café, sunny and invigorating work-spaces, and plenty of features our team enjoys. But we didn't stop there. We added a big slide in the middle of the building so everyone could remember to have fun throughout the day. Then, we literally took it to *a whole 'notha level*. We wanted a place where we could dream Leg-endary Dreams, so we added a fourth rooftop level—complete with an open-air fountain and a sunny dreaming space!

We did the same thing when we built our two-story hacienda at our cattle ranch. Cindy led the way on that project, working with experts to dream through the layout and design. But one feature I love is the third level we added that really makes it legendary. I love sitting up there with my family, watching thunderstorms roll across the Florida plains. It's another incredible dream space that has inspired even more Legendary Dreams.

One of my favorite memories at the haci-enda is when Cindy surprised me by inviting several of my former basketball players to join us at the ranch. Of course, they gave me a hard time for all the workouts I put them through back in that high school gym. But, more impor-tantly, as we sat together on that third level under the starry sky, they got to step into one of my dreams. They experienced firsthand the power of dreaming that night and saw what was possible for them if they dared to dream and redream at *a whole 'notha level.*

Dreaming at this Legendary level has caused me to see there is a lot of truth to the cliche "If you can dream it, you can do it." It's not always easy, but the first step to doing anything that hasn't been done before is to dream it. Without the dream, I guarantee no one will ever do whatever *it* is.

These days, we're daring to redream in legendary ways we never imagined possible. We're helping build schools and gymnasiums in struggling areas to give more children the opportunity to follow their dreams. Likewise, we're not only giving millions of dollars to support those affected by cancer, we're daring to dream of something more legendary. We want to find a cure for cancer. And we're getting involved in significant ways to help end human trafficking altogether.

These are Legendary Dreams—the kind that cause me to jump out of bed each morning, excited by what we will achieve by working with so many passionate and talented people around the world who are dedicated to the same cause.

As I look back, I am amazed at the number of times I've questioned whether I could achieve a Legendary Dream but pursued it anyway. What I have found in my own experience is that, when I trust God and pursue the crazy dreams He plants in my heart, somehow it all works out as I take action.

As your coach on this dream journey, I know this process works because I've lived it repeatedly. Every time I've achieved a dream, I've dared to work my Dream Muscle and redream until I can eventually dream at *a whole 'notha level*. And you can too. If you are willing to stretch your Dream Muscle and fully engage the Dream Phenomenon to redream again and again and never give up, you'll be amazed by the power of your dreams.

YOUR REDREAM STARTER QUESTIONS

You now have permission to redream. If you need some help, I have some Redream Starter Questions to help you reengage the Dream Phenomenon and keep yourself moving along the Dreamline.

The point of this exercise is to start thinking about what is calling to your heart and what you might dare to do in the future. I want you to dream and redream until you know you're chasing the kind of dreams you're afraid to say out loud.

Find your own dream space where you can think about these questions. Go somewhere that encourages you to dream or engage in an activity that helps inspire you to do seemingly impossible things. Take a journal or your phone to jot down or record your thoughts. You'll find it helpful to capture many of the ideas that start to flow through you, and you'll appreciate being able to review them later to see your progress.

Now, if you are ready, let's go! Ask yourself these questions to start redreaming and really listen to what is stirring within you:

1. If money were no object, what would I dare to do?
2. What thoughts about future possibilities keep me awake at night?
3. What would I love to be able to do for my family and those I care about?
4. What is one way I would like to change the world?
5. What am I too afraid to put on my Dream Board or even say out loud?

As your Dream Muscle strengthens, Legendary Dreams await. The best dreams are yet to come—if you're brave enough to dream again. You've heard my story. I've proven this works, and if I can do it—from teacher and coach to millionaire to billionaire—you can do it too.

YOUR DREAM PLAN

1. **Your Redream Starter.** By now, you've probably identified a Good Dream. Maybe you've even achieved your Good Dream at this point! Take a few minutes to think through the Redream Starter Questions and write your answers below.

   - If money were no object, what would you dare to do?

   - What thoughts about future possibilities keep you awake at night?

   - What would you love to be able to do for your family and those you care about?

   - What is one way you would like to change the world?

   - What were you too afraid to put on your Dream Board or even say out loud?

2. **Go to *a Whole 'Notha Level.*** What Legendary Dream is stirring deep within, living only in your wildest imagination? What dream might you pursue if you truly believed there were no limits to what is possible? What dream would you love to take to *a whole 'notha level*?

3. **Find Your Dream Space.** The best way to redream is to intentionally make time to do it in a space that encourages you to freely and easily dream. Where is that place for you? And why does that space encourage you to freely and easily dream?

   - Do you schedule time to dream? Think about your daily rhythms and when you could realistically unplug from the "to do" list and focus on "what could be."

4. **Your Dream Board 2.0.** Members of our It Works! family often create incredible Dream Boards when they join our company. But then, after a few short months, they realize they've already

achieved many of their dreams. When they create that first Dream Board, their Dream Muscles are just starting to move again. But as their muscles strengthen, they want to redream. They then revisit those boards and take their dreams to *a whole 'notha level.* You can expect to do the same thing. If you already have a Dream Board, keep it fresh with your latest dreams!

SECRET SAUCE

There is a reason you have the
dreams you do inside you.

I'd like to leave you with three final Secret Sauce recipes for living the life of your dreams.

SECRET SAUCE #1: LIVE IN THE DASH

It was a Friday evening. We were having one of our best years ever at It Works! We'd closed the office early so everyone could be part of a charity celebrity football game. I had planned on only coaching, but when some of our players got hurt, I saw an opportunity to get in the game with former University of Florida and NFL player Tim Tebow as my quarterback.

When we were in the huddle, I told Tim, "Look, I know this is a charity game, but I'm here to win!" He heard me. I caught three touchdown passes from him!

I felt awesome, especially when a younger guy from another team called to me, "Dude, you got wheels!"

"Sure," I shot back, still trying to catch my breath, "training wheels!" I was on a high as our team made it all the way to the finals. We had a blast! We gave back and had fun doing it.

That was Friday. On Monday morning, my phone rang as Cindy and I were eating breakfast. It was my doctor. I had gone in for a routine checkup with him the week before, so I didn't think much of it.

"Hey, Doc, what's the news?" I answered, finishing my last bite of breakfast as Cindy sat next to me.

"Mark," he said directly, "we've got a problem. Do you remember the extra test we ran last week as a precaution?"

"Yeah," I said, "of course." My face must have betrayed my concern because Cindy leaned toward me with a serious look.

"Well, that test is designed to check your heart, but it also detects multiple myeloma, a cancer that affects plasma cells," he explained.

I stayed quiet for a moment, thinking about what he was implying. I reached out for Cindy's hand and asked, "Doc, are you talking about me?"

"Yes, Mark. You have cancer."

After that call, the next season of my life was dedicated to treatments as I took everything day by day. Along the way, I learned that there is no complete cure for this type of cancer—yet. Thankfully, by God's grace and after extensive treatments, I am in remission and am getting regular checkups as I keep dreaming and moving forward.

The entire experience has focused my attention on this truth: There are two sets of numbers that really matter. The date on which you were born, and the date on which you die. In between the two is a dash (—). That's it. That's your life. A dash. If you are reading these words, it is where you are right now—*in the dash*. The truth is that none of us are promised tomorrow, but when cancer is staring you in the face, it gets real, real fast.

Each of us is living in that dash, and the second set of numbers is coming, so we need to make sure our time truly matters. So often, we put off our dreams for "another day." Living in the dash means we live each moment to the fullest, knowing we only have a limited amount of time here on this earth.

My cancer journey is a constant reminder to me that we can't wait to chase our dreams. My diagnosis lit a fire in me to dream more than ever, to celebrate milestones more, and to do more for others than I ever imagined possible. I've gotten more intentional about managing my energy levels, but I approach every day with a heightened sense of purpose and the urgency not to wait for "someday." I'm not looking to ride off into the sunset like many of my fictional cowboy heroes. I don't believe God created us to "retire." In fact, the very idea that I would ever retire from dreaming just fires me up even more!

Maybe you adjust or move into a different role as you age, but if God's given you the ability to dream, then He expects you to use it. On the other hand, perhaps you are young and in the prime of life. That second set of numbers may feel a long way off. I truly hope it is. But none of us really knows, so why would you wait to pursue your dream?

If God has given you the ability to dream and make a better life for others, why wouldn't you choose to get busy and do it? Choose to be a "dreamer of the day"—one of those people who dares to dream with their eyes wide open and achieve what others say is impossible.

The question is this: Are you willing to pursue the dreams planted in your heart and trust that they have been put there for greater reasons than you can ever know?

SECRET SAUCE #2: GIVE MORE TO GIVE MORE

You may have heard the expression "Give more to get more." People say it because there is an element of truth to it. When you give generously to help others, sometimes good things do come back to you. But that should never be *why* you give. I prefer to say, "Give more to *give* more." Because that's truly how it works. I've learned that the more you give, the more you end up being able to give.

To be honest, I don't like talking about what we give. It makes me uncomfortable. I don't want it to be about me or come across as some sort of humble-brag. At the same time, I've had people I look to for spiritual and life guidance tell me that I *should* be more open about what we give because giving is contagious. Their thought was that if people knew more about it, they may be inspired to dream and give more. My vulnerability might spark greater generosity in others—perhaps even in you.

I remember one winter evening when the kids were little. Cindy was still running the day care out of our house, and I was lining athletic fields while teaching. As we all sat around the dinner table, my daughter Kami asked, "Dad, one of my friends at school doesn't have a winter coat and gloves. Can we buy them a new coat and gloves?"

Now, the truth was that we didn't have money to buy new coats and gloves for our own children. Cindy did an amazing job of finding deals at garage sales to keep them clothed, but, even still, we had to find ways to stretch our budget. So the question caught me off guard—and broke my heart. Even though we didn't have the money to buy our own kids new things, we dug deep and found a way to help others and model generosity for our own children. At the same time, we could have done so much more *if* we would've had the money to do so.

I think of this as one of our early Good Dreams for giving. Having more cash than bills was about getting freedom to do more of the things that mattered to us. If it had been about money, we would've been satisfied a long time ago. But it's always been about how we can pursue our dreams in a way that helps more people.

In case you haven't noticed, there are some serious problems in the world that can keep you up at night. Several years ago, I attended a gala for the V Foundation, which helps kids who are fighting cancer. The organization was founded by my friend Dick Vitale, who has battled cancer himself for many years. That night, I saw little kids fighting for their lives to defeat cancer. But I learned that only 4 percent of the money for cancer research around the world was going to help kids. When I saw Dick giving his all for those kids, I thought, *I can't spend another day on this earth not fighting for those kids.*

I remember the first time I wrote a million-dollar check to the V Foundation. Back when we gave a couple of coats to kids, I never thought I would one day help so many other children by writing a check like that. If I had chosen to stay put in teaching, maybe I could have led a coat drive every winter to provide coats for some kids in our town. That would have been a Good Dream. But I kept dreaming and redreaming. Now, we've given many more millions to the V Foundation. Plus, we've connected them with the Moffitt Cancer Center to multiply each organization's impact, and we continue to fund cutting-edge research to cure cancer.

I'm still amazed that a former high school coach and teacher could now be in the position to give so much. But here's the thing: I believe it's why we were blessed in the first place. We committed to give more so we could ultimately give even more. I never imagined I could go from giving a couple of coats to funding the search for a cure for cancer. It happened because I never stopped dreaming.

Dick Vitale told me that when people achieve their dreams, they often forget where they came from and simply don't give back. I never want that to be me. And I don't want that for you. You may not be able to write a million-dollar check, but start where you are and follow your first giving dream. There have been so many times that we gave as a team by donating time or energy at shelters and community centers. Every bit of giving matters.

As you follow the Dream Phenomenon, you join our group of Active Dreamers who, I believe, will soon give back more than any of us can imagine. So, whatever you do, don't stop dreaming. And, as you give, look out! You'll do a lot of good in the world as your ability to give goes to *a whole 'notha level!*

SECRET SAUCE #3: KNOW WHEN ENOUGH IS ENOUGH

As I've pursued the dreams planted in my heart, I occasionally get asked, "When is enough enough?"

On the one hand, I get it. Some people might think we've had enough success. On the other hand, when I first heard that question, I got a little defensive. I thought it implied that I was greedy and pursuing my dreams for the wrong reasons. To be honest, there *is* a lot of greed in our world today, so it's always good to check our motives.

But it really got me thinking, *When* is *enough enough?* The American Dream is not all about money. It's about having the freedom and opportunity to create a better life for yourself and those you love. As you've read, I'm living proof that the American Dream is alive and well. If this coach and teacher with blue-collar roots can pursue dreams that produce such abundance and impact the lives of others in such positive ways, anyone can. I don't have any special talents or skills that others don't. I simply worked out my Dream Muscle as I followed the Dream Phenomenon:

1. I gave myself permission to **Get in the Game** and pursue what mattered to me.
2. I **Spoke and Saw** my dreams clearly so I could achieve them.
3. I **Lived on the Offense,** making risk my friend.
4. I always **Got Back Up** as I engaged in work that was worth it.
5. I **Found My People** who could help my dreams thrive.
6. I **Celebrated My Wins** along the way (often with crazy end-zone dances!).
7. I always **Dared to Redream** and take my dreams to *a whole 'notha level!*

So after initially getting a little defensive when someone asked when enough is enough, I reconsidered my response and went on the offense. I began to think of all the good we've been able to do in the world because of the success of our dreams.

I thought about how many thousands upon thousands of hours and millions of dollars we've donated to so many worthy causes.

I thought about the hundreds of thousands of people who have worked with our company, improved themselves, and enabled their families to enjoy more fun and financial freedom.

I considered how the Dream Ripples we create will reach far beyond my own life and touch many generations to come.

With all that in mind, I gave my answer: "I guess enough will be enough when everyone is dreaming again, when poverty is no longer a reality for billions of people, when no more people are enslaved in human trafficking, and when we've finally found a cure for cancer. Maybe then that will be enough."

I honestly wasn't trying to be harsh, but the question forced me to focus on why I keep pursuing my dreams. It isn't about me. It isn't about making money. Money is just a way to measure value delivered to the rest of the world. And making money has never been the ultimate goal for us. It's about making the world a better place.

I share this with you because, if you're chasing your dreams, you'll likely get the same question at some point: *When is enough enough?* When you hear it, your first response might be to get defensive like I did, to start questioning your motives, or feel like you're in the wrong. You might even be tempted to quit dreaming.

But here's why you shouldn't do any of those things: *The world needs your dreams.* If you get nothing else from this book, I trust you hear this loud and clear: *You were born to dream.* There is a reason you have the dreams you do inside you. My faith in God—my core drive to dream—tells me that reason has a lot to do with God's plan for your life.

I believe dreaming big isn't selfish, especially when God is steering you. Dreaming for me is actually about being able to give back what has been given to us and seeing His will be done on earth as it is in heaven. So as long as I have breath in me, I hope I never stop dreaming. I want to go *all out* and keep giving more to the world until my time here is done.

You and I likely haven't met in person, at least not yet. I hope one day we do because I know you're a dreamer. I know you have the potential to do a lot of good in the world and to accomplish amazing things with your dreams. But, at the end of the day, it's up to you.

You can choose to let fear restrict your Dream Muscle, or you can choose to keep building on the momentum you've created as you've read. I sincerely hope you choose to keep dreaming, because I can't wait to hear about all the good your dreams do!

So, what are you waiting for? Go—live the life of your dreams!

NOTES

1. Gallup International Association, "Less Hope and Happiness in the World 2021," D.N.S. Werbe GmbH, December 28, 2021, https://www.gallup -international.com/survey-results-and-news/survey -result/less-hope-and-happiness-in-the-world-2021.

2. Koichiro Shiba et al. "Purpose in Life and 8-Year Mortality by Gender and Race/Ethnicity Among Older Adults in the U.S," *Preventive Medicine* 164 (2022): 107310, https://doi.org/10.1016/j.ypmed .2022.107310; Koichiro Shiba et al., "Associations Between Purpose in Life and Mortality by SES," *American Journal of Preventive Medicine* 61, no. 2 (2021): e53–e61, https://doi.org/10.1016/j.amepre .2021.02.011.

3. Health and Retirement Study Survey Research Center, "The Health and Retirement Study," The Regents of the University of Michigan, 2023, https:// hrs.isr.umich.edu/.

4. Eric S. Kim, Shelley D. Hershner, and Victor J. Strecher, "Purpose in Life and Incidence of Sleep

Disturbances," *Journal of Behavioral Medicine* 38 (2015): 590–97, https://doi.org/10.1007/s10865-015 -9635-4.

5. Eric S. Kim et al., "Purpose in Life and Reduced Incidence of Stroke in Older Adults: 'The Health and Retirement Study,'" *Journal of Psychosomatic Research* 74, no. 5 (2013): 427–32, https://doi.org /10.1016/j.jpsychores.2013.01.013.

6. Patrick E. McKnight and Todd B. Kashdan, "Purpose in Life as a System That Creates and Sustains Health and Well-Being: An Integrative, Testable Theory," *Review of General Psychology* 13, no. 3 (2009): 242–51, https://doi.org/10.1037/a0017152.

7. Dr. Dan Vosgerichian, "Use Visualization, Imagery Like Many of Golf's Greats," Golf WRX, October 13, 2013, https://www.golfwrx.com/140719/use -visualization-imagery-like-many-of-golfs-greats/.

8. Shahzad Tahmasebi Boroujeni and Mehdi Shahbazi, "The Effect of Instructional and Motivational Self-Talk on Performance of Basketball's Motor Skill," *Procedia—Social and Behavioral Sciences* 15 (2011): 3113–17, https://doi.org/10.1016/j.sbspro.2011.04 .255.

9. Edwin A. Locke and Gary P. Latham, "New Directions in Goal-Setting Theory," *Current Directions in Psychological Science* 15, no. 5 (2006): 265–68, https://doi.org/10.1111/j.1467-8721.2006.00449.x.

10. "Neural Pathways: How Your Mind Stores the Info and Thoughts That Affect Your Behaviour," lifeXchange, accessed January 13, 2025, https://lifexchangesolutions.com/neural-pathways/.

11. Lara Doherty, "The Science Behind Vision Boards," The Motivation Clinic, November 1. https://www.themotivationclinic.co.uk/blog/blog-post-title-three-grwe9.

12. The Associated Press, "How Hard Is It to Win the Lottery? Odds to Keep in Mind as Powerball and Mega Millions Jackpots Soar," AP News, July 19, 2023, https://apnews.com/article/powerball-mega-millions-winning-odds-numbers-a3e5a8e8e7ed15d7500c1d6acdab6785.

13. "Thoughts on the Business of Life," Forbes Quotes, accessed January 13, 2025, https://www.forbes.com/quotes/11194/.

14. Rob Cross, Karen Dillon, and Danna Greenberg, "The Secret to Building Resilience," *Harvard Business Review*, January 29, 2021, https://hbr.org/2021/01/the-secret-to-building-resilience.

15. Lydia Denworth, "Synchronized Minds," *Scientific American* 329, no. 1 (July/August 2023): 50, https://doi.org/10.1038/scientificamerican0723-50.

16. Kyongsik Yun, Katsumi Watanabe, and Shinsuke Shimojo, "Interpersonal Body and Neural Synchronization as a Marker of Implicit Social Interaction,"

Scientific Reports 2, article no. 959 (2012), https://doi.org/10.1038/srep00959.

17. Judith E. Glaser, "Celebration Time: A Cocktail Each Executive Should Know How to Mix," *Psychology Today*, December 28, 2015, https://www.psychology today.com/us/blog/conversational-intelligence/2015 12/celebration-time.

18. BJ Fogg, "How You Can Use the Power of Celebration to Make New Habits Stick," IDEAS.TED.COM, January 6, 2020, https://ideas.ted.com/how-you-can-use-the-power-of-celebration-to-make-new-habits-stick/.

19. Benjamin Cheyette M.D. and Sarah Cheyette M.D., "Why It's Important to Celebrate Small Successes: One Simple Habit Can Build a Lifetime of Motivation," *Psychology Today*, November 22, 2021. https://www.psychologytoday.com/us/blog/1-2-3-adhd/202111/why-its-important-celebrate-small-successes.

In the following pages, I would like to share a few of my favorite quotes to remind you to live the life of your dreams. I encourage you to share any that resonate with you—please follow and tag me on social media!

 Mark.Pentecost.14

TheMarkPentecost

 MarkbPentecost

 MarkbPentecost

"PEOPLE ARE OFTEN SCARED OF DOING THE WRONG THING WHEN WHAT THEY SHOULD BE SCARED OF IS DOING NOTHING."

— MARK PENTECOST

"THE DAY YOU START DREAMING
IS THE DAY YOU START LIVING."

— MARK PENTECOST

"IF YOU DON'T RISK FOR SOMETHING DIFFERENT, YOU GUARANTEE MORE OF THE SAME."

— MARK PENTECOST

"THERE'S NO SUCH THING AS WORK THAT IS HARD, ONLY WORK THAT IS WORTH IT."

— MARK PENTECOST

"WHEN PLANTED IN THE RIGHT ENVIRONMENT, DREAMS THRIVE. WHEN PLANTED IN THE WRONG ENVIRONMENT, DREAMS DIE."

— MARK PENTECOST

"CELEBRATIONS SHOULD HAPPEN AT MILESTONES, NOT JUST DESTINATIONS."

— MARK PENTECOST

"THE DREAM THAT WILL MAKE YOU
MOST PROUD IS THE ONE YOU'RE
AFRAID TO SAY OUT LOUD."

— MARK PENTECOST